Richard M. Foxx

INCREASING BEHAVIORS

of Persons With Severe Retardation and Autism

RESEARCH PRESS
2612 North Mattis Avenue
Champaign, Illinois 61821

To Carolyn for all of her personal support and professional suggestions throughout the years

CONTENTS

PREFACE

This volume is the first of two books for practitioners covering increasing and decreasing the behaviors of severely and profoundly retarded and autistic individuals. This book is intended to provide the reader with a behavioral foundation and thus is less complex than its companion volume on decreasing behaviors. This hierarchical arrangement was by design, since there is a strong tendency on the part of practitioners to decrease rather than build behavior. Yet if prosocial and developmentally appropriate behaviors are increased first, the behavioral programmer is left with fewer behaviors that must be decreased. Thus, readers should first master this material before turning to the other book.

This book is intended for teachers, aides, institutional staff, parents, and persons responsible for designing or evaluating behavioral programs. It is not intended for individuals with an extensive background in behavioral principles, although they may find it useful as an aid in training others. I did not endeavor to write a scholarly book because there already exist a number of excellent ones; nor have I tried to oversimplify the behavioral approach by using a recipe format, since that too has been done. Rather, I have tried to bridge the gap between the esoteric scientific world and the pragmatic applied world.

Accordingly, I set the following guidelines. (1) Only crucial information would be included. (2) A problem-solving approach, rather than a cookbook approach, would be emphasized. (3) Information would be interrelated wherever possible in order to stress concepts and avoid the compartmentalization that is common in texts of this type. (4) Caveats would be provided that are scientifically based, yet rarely, if ever, provided in training manuals. (5) It would be emphasized that the behavior of handicapped students is lawful and thereby explainable. In effect, I wanted to stress that behavior occurs on a continuum so that readers could appreciate that they are influenced by the same principles that affect their students.

I have attempted to present the material in a logical sequence that gradually increases in complexity. It begins with how to determine what behaviors are to be increased, then explains how to increase them, followed by how to arrange and manipulate the learning environment, how to use various techniques for facilitating acquisition, and how to evaluate success and then maintain it. The inclusion of frequent quizzes should help readers master each section before they proceed. In this way I have tried to use the very principles that are presented by shaping the reader's behavioral skills while at the same time ensuring that the material is successfully mastered.

The material is presented in nontechnical language wherever possible to maximize its readability. I have tried to strike a fine balance between preserving the technical jargon that must be learned while keeping the material as interesting, relevant, and informative as possible. As a further aid, a practical glossary has been included that defines the various technical terms used throughout the book. I have taken liberty in defining some of the terms because I have found in over 200 workshops presented to thousands of people that individuals unfamiliar with behavioral principles learn and comprehend the terms best when they are defined more simply.

A couple of explanations are in order. First, the term "student" is used throughout the text even though the various examples reflect residential, home, and classroom situations. The selection of this term was purposeful since it conveys the spirit of educating and training, whereas terms such as "client" and "resident" do not. To me, everyone entrusted with the care of the handicapped is first and foremost a teacher. This also explains the frequent use of the term "teacher" even though the described situation may involve an aide, therapist, psychologist, nurse, or other practitioner. Second, I chose to focus on the severely and profoundly retarded because there are few texts available that deal with these individuals. Appropriate programming for these individuals requires more expertise than for mildly retarded individuals because of their special learning problems and their increased need for the use of specialized behavioral techniques such as shaping, fading, and backward chaining. Furthermore, although the focus is on retarded individuals, most of the material is applicable to those autistic individuals who share the same deficits as their retarded counterparts.

Several people were of assistance with this book. First and foremost, my wife, Carolyn, critically read each chapter and provided excellent, detailed feedback as well as co-authoring Chapter 1 and the task analysis section in Chapter 9. Her contributions were especially helpful and valued because she has had extensive experience in teaching behavior modification skills to institutional staff, parents, and college students, as well as in directing an institutional-based program for problem residents. Marty McMorrow and Reed Bechtel critically read and commented on the material and assisted in compiling the suggested readings. In addition, Marty helped compile the glossary and assisted with technical matters. Ellen Morgan provided accurate transcriptions of seemingly incomprehensible handwritten materials, and Ron Bittle, superintendent of the Anna Mental Health and Developmental Center, provided his customary advice and support that I have come to value so highly over the years. Finally, I would like to thank the many individuals throughout the country who have shared their experiences and insights with me during my visits to their programs.

Richard M. Foxx
Anna, Illinois

CHAPTER 1

Behavioral Objectives

The behavioral approach is based on the direct observation of a student's behavior. When we directly observe a behavior, we can describe it fully by specifying what the action is and when, where, and how often it occurs. Furthermore, the behavioral approach has us break down behaviors into small observable units that allow everyone concerned with the student's education to objectively measure them and thereby agree on which behaviors are or are not occurring. In this way, the behavioral approach provides a scientifically based method for teaching the retarded student new behaviors.

To use the behavioral model effectively, you must develop the skills to think, write, and speak in a clear, precise, and complete way. Learning how to write descriptive statements called *behavioral objectives* is a simple way of achieving these skills. In this chapter we will show you the three components of a behavioral objective and teach you how to recognize and write objectives that are complete, meaningful, and realistic.

THE COMPONENTS OF A BEHAVIORAL OBJECTIVE

A behavioral objective is a written statement that describes three things about an individual's performance of a behavior: (1) what the behavior is, (2) how much or how well it is done, and (3) the circumstances under which it is done.

A good behavioral objective must have three components. First, the behavior the student will perform must be stated precisely in observable, measurable terms. Second, a description of how that behavior will be measured must be included, for ex-

1

ample, how much, how long, or how well it is to be done. In other words, a *criterion level* of performance must be specified. Third, the exact circumstances in which the behavior will be performed must be stated.

Writing good behavioral objectives is not as simple as it seems; in fact, it requires a good deal of practice. Let's consider each of the three components separately.

Stating What the Behavior Is

We'll begin with the *behavioral verb*, the description of the measurable behavior the student will be expected to perform. A behavioral verb always describes an observable action. Some examples are:

brushes	draws	looks at	sits
chews	eats	points to	stacks
climbs	feeds self	pulls	strings
combs	holds	pushes	swallows
cries	jumps	runs	talks
dances	lifts	says	walks

Some examples of verbs that are *not* behavioral but that are often mistakenly used in writing instructional objectives or goals are the following:

appreciates	is aware of
cares	knows
enjoys	likes
has ability to	respects
has idea of	understands

Behavioral verbs aren't subject to interpretation, whereas nonbehavioral verbs require interpretation and a value judgment. A behavioral verb clearly tells you what the student will do. (Note that this is in contrast to the way educators have traditionally specified instructional goals by stating what the teacher would do; for example, "Teach gross motor skills to Jim" or "Teach dressing skills to Arthur.") Furthermore, a behavioral verb describes the behavior to be performed in such a way that it can be seen and measured by two or more people.

The importance of stating the behavior in active, measurable terms cannot be overemphasized. Otherwise there may be some confusion concerning what the student is supposed to do. If a teacher only says, "Carl will display good listening skills," her aide may well have no clear idea of what Carl is to do.

Practice Set 1A

Place a check mark beside each of the following statements that includes a good behavioral verb. (Remember, the verb should not be subject to interpretation.)

_____ 1. Mary combs her hair.

_____ 2. Bobby likes his music therapy class.

_____ 3. John walks to the toilet.

_____ 4. Mimi knows appropriate table manners.

_____ 5. Dorothy appreciates attention.

The answers are on page 187.

Stating the Criterion Level

A behavioral objective should not only precisely specify the student's behavior in measurable terms, but it should also state the criteria or criterion level for acceptable performance. Thus, we must decide how to measure the student's behavior in such a way that we know that the objective has been met.

This brings us to the second component, which is the *criterion level of performance*, a description of how much or how well the behavior is to be performed. Here is a list of some behavioral verbs that are followed by several potential performance criteria.

Behavioral Verb	Criterion Level of Performance
Combs hair	without assistance within 5 minutes until hair is free of tangles
Claps hands	with fingers extended three times
Walks to toilet	without assistance within 10 minutes after lunch trays are removed from unit
Eats meals	using spoon without spilling food on clothing or table without finishing within 10 minutes of serving time
Signs for teacher's attention	only after task is completed before leaving table
Makes eye contact	on at least 9 of 10 requested trials

From these examples it's apparent that there are four common ways to set a criterion level. The first is to specify a time limit during which the behavior must be completed. A second is to specify the number of repetitions of the behavior that must be performed. A third way is to specify a qualitative, yet measurable, level of performance, e.g., "hair free of tangles" or "without assistance." Finally, a fourth way is to specify an accuracy level, e.g., "eye contact will occur on 90% of the trials."

Practice Set 1B

Place a check mark beside each of the following objectives that contains an observable and measurable criterion level of performance.

_____ 1. John will pour juice into a glass.

_____ 2. Francis will hold a cup in one hand for 5 seconds.

_____ 3. Carolyn will only use a spoon to feed herself.

_____ 4. Bruce will hang up his coat within 2 minutes after entering the classroom.

_____ 5. Dot will shower herself.

Answers are found on page 187.

Stating the Conditions

The third component of a good behavioral objective is *a statement of the exact conditions* or circumstances in which the behavior is to be performed. Writing a behavioral objective without specifying the conditions under which the behavior is to be performed can lead to confusion. For example, consider the following objective: Madi will eat her entire meal with a spoon. A behavioral verb, *eat*, was used. The criterion level of performance was specified, that is, *Madi* will eat her *entire* meal with a *spoon*. Yet many questions are left unanswered that would make it difficult to evaluate whether or not the objective had been achieved. For example, we don't know if Madi will receive physical guidance from her instructor, or use the spoon without being instructed to do so. Thus we must specify the conditions in which Madi must perform eating with a spoon: "When given a spoon and instructions to use it, Madi will eat her entire meal with a spoon."

The conditions in a behavioral objective are the "givens" associated with the performance of the behavior: how, when, where, with what, or with whom. They are the setting in which the behavior occurs. Some examples include required instructions, necessary equipment, and the appropriate time and place for the behavior to appear. Here are some examples of conditions under which a behavior must be performed.

Behavioral Verb	Criterion Level	Conditions
Combs hair	without assistance within 5 minutes until free of tangles	before going to lunch when instructed to do so after showering

Claps hands	with fingers
	  extended
	three times
	
	when told to do so
		while teacher plays
		  piano
		when instructed by
		  aide
		without physical
		  guidance

Walks to toilet	without assistance
	within 10 minutes
	  after lunch trays
	  are removed from
	  unit
	when instructed to
	  do so
		before boarding bus
		when instructed to
		  do so
		
		using walker

Eats meals	using spoon
	without spilling
	  food on clothing
	  or table
	without finishing
	  within 10 minutes
	  of serving time
		without spilling food
		when hand is guided
		  by teacher
		
		during lunch period

Signs for teacher's
attention
	only after task is
	  completed
	before leaving table
	during free time
	  activity
		during sorting task
		
		in the dining room
		when teacher is not
		  with another
		  student

It may occur to you that some conditions are no different than performance criteria. For example, if someone is to finish her lunch "within 30 minutes," you may ask yourself whether this is the set of conditions under which the behavior is to occur or a statement of the performance criterion for the behavior. In this case, the answer is both! Sometimes when a behavior is performed under a certain set of conditions it's also meeting the criterion or criteria requirements as well. Other times there may be a clear distinction between the performance criteria and conditions; for instance, "Given a five-piece puzzle (condition), Carrie will complete (behavioral verb) the puzzle within 1 minute (criterion level)." Because of the infinite number of potential behavioral objectives, there is no simple formula that can be given regarding how to distinguish between every set of criteria and conditions. Thus, it is the writer of the behavioral objective who must decide which particular aspects of a situation would qualify as the criteria and which as the conditions for the performance of the behavior.

THE CONSTRUCTION OF GOOD BEHAVIORAL OBJECTIVES

You don't need to pack every little detail you can think of into a behavioral objective. In fact, such an objective might leave you lost in a mass of irrelevant information. Consider how confusing the following objective is because of the inclusion of unnecessary information: "Given a five-piece puzzle of a horse placed before her on a table, Carrie, while seated, will complete the puzzle within 1 minute using both hands."

What is important is that you keep the objectives simple yet complete. Because you know your students and what you want them to accomplish, it's up to you to decide which particular aspects of the learning situation are necessary to accomplish the objective. As a guide, ask the following questions when you are constructing your behavioral objective:

1. What behavior do you want the student to perform? (behavioral verb)
2. How well should the student perform this behavior? (criterion level)
3. Under what circumstances do you expect the student to perform this behavior? (learning conditions)

Practice Set 1C

For each objective, place a check mark in the appropriate column if it contains that component. If all three columns are checked, the statement is a good behavioral objective.

	Contains Behavioral Verb	Has Measurable Criterion Level	Specifies Necessary Conditions
1. When instructed, Ben will raise his pants to his waist on 9 out of 10 trials.			

	Contains Behavioral Verb	Has Measurable Criterion Level	Specifies Necessary Conditions
2. Mimi will tie her shoes.			
3. Given a towel, the student will know how to use it.			
4. When given a fork, the student will independently feed himself.			
5. Given a crayon and paper, Gigi will draw circles.			
6. The student will brush her teeth for 2 minutes when physical prompts are provided.			

The answers are on pages 187 and 188.

While it's relatively easy to compose a behavioral objective that meets the three component requirements already described, it's often difficult to ensure that an objective is meaningful and realistically attainable. Meaningful and realistic behavioral objectives should specify a behavior (1) that the student doesn't already perform successfully, (2) that is relevant and thereby useful in the environment in which the student lives and is expected to function, (3) that would be the next logical, developmental step, and (4) that is achievable.

Many objectives that are written don't meet these criteria and thus are meaningless. For example, if Joe already ties his shoes independently, why write an objective to teach him this skill? Why write an objective to teach Mary to identify three colors when she has not yet mastered any of the basic self-help skills? Developmentally speaking, how can Conrad be expected to utter a simple sentence when he has just learned to imitate sounds? Or why write an objective that Tony will feed himself independently when he has no motor control over his arms and no suitable prosthetic device has been developed as yet to give him this control?

To ensure that your proposed behavioral objectives meet these four criteria you should (1) perform an adequate assessment of the student's current level of functioning as it relates to the objective,

(2) determine whether or not the student even *needs* to be able to perform that behavior or skill, (3) make certain that the objective makes sense developmentally in that the student is capable of accomplishing it at this time, and (4) determine whether the student will ever be capable of accomplishing the objective.

The development of good behavioral objectives can be quite complex. In fact, whole books have been devoted to the subject, since instructional or behavioral objectives are written for all levels of education. In this book we have merely presented a relatively short discussion so that you can begin working on developing good behavioral objectives. If you want to study this area in more depth, you might try any of the suggested readings at the end of the chapter.

SUMMARY

The most effective techniques for teaching retarded students come from the behavioral model, a scientifically based approach that relies on direct observation. This model requires you to pinpoint what and how the student is to learn by creating behavioral objectives. These objectives describe the student's behavior, rather than the teacher's, and are useful tools for planning and evaluating the student's educational goals.

A good behavioral objective contains three components: (1) a behavioral verb (action) that states what behavior the student will perform, (2) a criterion level of acceptable performance, which can be stated as a time limit, a number of repetitions, a qualitative level, or an accuracy level, and (3) the exact conditions or circumstances under which the behavior will be performed.

Good objectives should also be simple but complete, and meaningful and realistic for the student. A meaningful and realistic behavioral objective will specify a behavior (1) that the student doesn't already perform successfully, (2) that is relevant and thereby useful in the environment in which the student lives and is expected to function, (3) that would be the next logical, developmental step, and (4) that is achievable.

SUGGESTED READINGS

Mager, R. F. *Preparing instructional objectives.* Belmont, Calif.: Pitman Learning, 1975.
Mager, R. F. *Goal analysis.* Belmont, Calif.: Fearon Pitman Publishers, 1972.

Sulzer-Azaroff, B., & Mayer, G. R. *Applying behavior analysis procedures with children and youth.* New York: Holt, Rinehart & Winston, 1977.

Vargas, J. S. *Writing worthwhile behavioral objectives.* New York: Harper & Row, 1972.

Review Set 1

1. The behavioral approach is based on the direct o_____ of a student's behavior.

2. A b_____ verb describes an observable action and is the first component of a behavioral objective.

3. The second component of a behavioral objective is setting a c_____ level of performance.

4. The third component of a behavioral objective is to state the exact c_____ or circumstances in which the behavior is to be performed.

5. Criterion levels regarding how the behavior must be performed can specify a t_____ limit, a number of r_____, a qualitative level of performance, or an a_____ level.

6. Understandable, useful behavioral objectives are kept s_____ but complete.

7. Meaningful and realistic behavioral objectives are characterized by specifying a behavior (a) that the student doesn't already p_____ successfully, (b) that is relevant and useful in the e_____ in which the student lives, (c) that would be the next logical, d_____ step, and (d) that is a_____.

The answers are on page 188.

CHAPTER 2

The Instructional Cycle or Three-Term Contingency

You now know how to write behavioral objectives so you have clear goals for your teaching. But in order for your students to attain the objectives you set for them, you need to understand the *instructional cycle* or three-term contingency. In this chapter, you'll learn about the three elements of the instructional cycle and how they relate to one another in forming a blueprint for instruction. We'll also explain what reinforcing and punishing consequences are and how they can be used in your teaching. By the end of this chapter you should be able to write an instructional cycle for teaching a new behavior or maintaining an old one.

THE ELEMENTS OF THE INSTRUCTIONAL CYCLE

There are three elements in the instructional cycle: a stimulus, a response, and a consequence.

The Stimulus

> A stimulus is any physical object or occurrence in the environment that may set the occasion for a response to occur.

The first element in the instructional cycle is the *stimulus*, which precedes the response and may set the occasion for a response to occur. A stimulus can be any physical object or occurrence (any event) in the environment. A few of the numerous stimuli in your instructional area are toys, tables, people, a verbal instruction, and a demonstration of some sort.

The importance of any particular stimulus is that it may cue a particular response. Knowing this relation between the stimulus and response lets us predict with some confidence what the student is likely to do. For example, we may observe that whenever a tray of food is placed in front of Sam, he lifts the tray and throws it across the room. Placing the tray of food in front of Sam is a physical occurrence (stimulus) in the environment that precedes and sets the occasion for Sam's response of throwing the tray. He couldn't throw the tray if it weren't in front of him to act as a stimulus. As a result, we can predict with assurance that placing a tray of food in front of Sam will lead to his throwing the tray. Having made this analysis, we can take steps to stop Sam's tray throwing.

It also could be that whenever a tray of food is placed in front of Sam, he picks up his spoon. In this case, the stimulus (the tray of food in front of Sam) precedes and sets the occasion for Sam's response of picking up his spoon. Thus, we can say that the tray of food is a stimulus that will lead to picking up a spoon.

Listed below are examples of various stimuli that you might find in your classroom or living unit and the responses that they are likely to cue. Remember, stimuli can be objects, people, happenings, or your instructions.

Stimulus	Response
A mirror on a table	Bob looks at himself.
A goldfish in a fishbowl	Ellen sticks her hand in the fishbowl.
A toy on a table	Sue throws the toy.
Feces in her diaper	Donna smears feces.
A rocking chair	Ted rocks in the chair.
A refrigerator	Alvin opens the refrigerator door to hunt for food.
"Steven, stand up."	Steven rises from his chair and stands up.
An open classroom door	Marty runs out of the classroom.
A staff member wearing glasses	John grabs the glasses.
A teacher claps her hands	Billy claps his hands.

Practice Set 2A

Read each of the following statements and determine the stimulus for each situation. Then fill in the stimulus.

1. Peter cried after Mr. Rendleman said, "It is time to catch the bus."

   The stimulus was _____

2. Susan pulled a button off her dress.

   The stimulus was _____

3. James walked over to the big wheel and sat on it.

   The stimulus was _____

4. When Ginger saw the needle she began to scream.

   The stimulus was _____

5. Robby picked up five pieces of candy.

   The stimulus was _____

The answers are on page 188.

The Response

> A response is the behavior the student performs in
> the presence of a particular stimulus.

The second element in the instructional cycle is the *response*, or behavior that follows the stimulus. (The terms response and behavior will be used interchangeably throughout this book.) Some common responses include sitting, walking, crying, talking, grasping a ball, biting, and tearing. The importance of the relation between a stimulus and a response cannot be overstressed. When you understand this relation, you can design programs to either increase or decrease a response. The following two examples demonstrate the wide variety of stimulus-response relations.

At a barbecue on the lawn outside the institutional living unit, a staff member gives Dorothy, a profoundly retarded student, a succulent hamburger and Dorothy eats it. Eating the hamburger was Dorothy's response to being given the hamburger, which served as the stimulus for eating. If Dorothy hadn't been given the hamburger, she wouldn't have had the opportunity to perform the response of eating it.

Back on the living unit, Dorothy smears her feces each time she defecates in her pants. Smearing her feces is her response to the presence of the feces in her pants. If the feces weren't present, there would be nothing for Dorothy to smear.

Listed here are examples of various stimuli and the particular responses that are performed in the presence of these stimuli.

Later in this chapter you'll learn that it is the consequences that follow these responses (behaviors) that maintain them.

Stimulus	Response
A glass of apple juice	Joe *drinks* the juice.
A jar of paste on the table	Sue *eats* paste.
Music playing	George *sways* to the music.
A newspaper	Benny *tears* the paper.
A roll of Christmas wrapping paper	Jessie *unrolls* the paper.
A dog wagging its tail	Timmy *grabs* the dog's tail.

Practice Set 2B

Read each of the following statements and determine the stimulus and response for each situation. Then fill in the stimulus and response.

1. Judy began to cry when her mother entered the play yard.

    Stimulus: _____

    Response: _____

2. Adam fell to the floor when Ms. Klein told him to stop pinching Sandy.

    Stimulus: _____

    Response: _____

3. Mary opened her mouth when the aide put a spoon near it.

    Stimulus: _____

    Response: _____

4. When Nate was in the bathroom, he began to drink from the toilet.

    Stimulus: _____

    Response: _____

The answers are on page 188.

The Consequence

> The consequence is the event that happens to the student after the response occurs.

The third element in the instructional cycle is the *consequence*, which is an event that follows the response. In other words, the consequence is what happens to the student after she has responded.

Sometimes the consequence is a natural event. For example, Dottie sees a bright light burning and is attracted to it. She edges toward the light bulb and reaches up and touches the hot bulb. The bulb burns her finger and she begins to cry. The stimulus in this situation was the bright light bulb, the response was touching it, and the consequence that followed the response was a burned finger. This consequence was a natural event because it was produced by the environment. Such natural consequences, whether negative or positive, are a part of our everyday world. As such, they have an effect on the way we behave.

There is another type of consequence that plays an even greater part in determining how we behave each day. These consequences are the ones that other people in the environment deliberately arrange to follow our behavior. They do so because they want to have an effect on our future behavior. Any intervention program that you design, whether it is to increase or decrease a behavior, must primarily concentrate on the development of consequences that will produce the desired effect on the behavior.

Listed here are examples of various stimuli, the particular responses that are performed in the presence of these stimuli, and the consequences that follow these responses.

Stimulus	Response	Consequence
A window on the living unit	Vickie *breaks* the window.	A staff member scolds Vickie.
A puzzle piece	Riley *inserts* the piece into a puzzle.	The teacher praises Riley.
Barbara's hair	Carol *pulls* Barbara's hair.	Barbara cries.
A pair of pants	Bruce *puts* the pants on.	The aide praises Bruce.
"Look at me."	Ellen *looks* at her teacher.	The teacher gives Ellen a slice of apple.

Practice Set 2C

Read each of the following statements and determine the stimulus, response, and consequence for each situation. Then fill in the stimulus, response, and consequence.

1. Mindy begins throwing toys. The instructor rushes over and grabs Mindy's hands to prevent her from throwing any more toys.

   Stimulus: _____

   Response: _____

   Consequence: _____

2. Daniel hands his teacher a toy when she asks him for it. His teacher tells him he is a good boy.

   Stimulus: _____

   Response: _____

   Consequence: _____

3. Helen picks at a scab on her hand. Each time the instructor sees her pick the scab, he tells her to stop.

   Stimulus: _____

   Response: _____

   Consequence: _____

4. Marvin throws his paper cup during the juice break. The instructor tells Marvin to sit in the corner.

   Stimulus: _____

   Response: _____

   Consequence: _____

5. Richard mouths his paint brush during an art activity. Each time the instructor catches him mouthing the brush, she takes him to the sink and rinses his mouth with water.

   Stimulus: _____

   Response: _____

   Consequence: _____

Answers are found on pages 188 and 189.

Now let's look at two situations in which the stimulus and the response are identical but the consequences are quite different.

The instructor places a Ping-Pong ball on Judy's desk. Judy bends down, purses her lips, and blows the ball toward her instructor, who is seated across from her. The instructor says, "Good, Judy, good blowing the ball" and gives her a piece of peanut butter cookie.

The instructor places a Ping-Pong ball on Brian's desk. Brian bends down, purses his lips, and blows the ball toward his instructor, who is seated across from him. The instructor says, "No, Brian, don't blow the ball" and then turns away from Brian for a minute.

In these two situations, the stimuli were the same (the Ping-Pong ball), as were the responses (blowing the ball), but the consequences were much different. The consequences Judy received were praise and a bite of her favorite cookie. The instructor wanted Judy to receive a pleasant consequence because she was supposed to blow the Ping-Pong ball. By doing so, Judy was strengthening her mouth and throat muscles, which was very important because, according to her physical therapist, Judy drooled because her mouth and throat muscles were weak. The consequences that Brian received were being reprimanded and ignored by his instructor. The instructor wanted Brian to receive an unpleasant consequence because he was supposed to hand the ball to the instructor rather than blow it. It was important for the instructor to discourage Brian because Brian often misbehaved in instructional sessions by blowing lightweight objects at his instructor.

These two situations illustrate an extremely important point: the type of consequence that is delivered following a behavior is determined by the effect the instructor wants to have on the future occurrence of the behavior. If the instructor wants the behavior to increase or continue, then she arranges for a pleasant consequence to follow the behavior. If, on the other hand, she wants the behavior to decrease or cease, she arranges for an unpleasant consequence to follow the behavior. Regardless of which choice the instructor makes, the future behavior or response will be affected by the consequence. This is why we say that *behavior is a function of its consequences*.

As you may have surmised, there are two basic types of consequences, *reinforcing* consequences and *punishing* consequences. When a reinforcing consequence follows a response or behavior, that response will *increase* in frequency, that is, it will occur more often in the future. When a punishing consequence follows a response, that response will *decrease* in frequency, that is, it will occur less often in the future.

In the previous examples, Judy's blowing response was followed by reinforcing consequences, praise and a bite of her favorite cookie, whereas Brian's blowing response was followed by punishing consequences, being reprimanded and ignored. We refer to the relation between Judy's behavior and the reinforcing consequences as *reinforcement* and the reinforcing consequences as *reinforcers* because they strengthen a behavior. We refer to the relation between Brian's behavior and the punishing consequences as *punishment* and the punishing consequences as *punishers* because they weaken a behavior.

Through the use of reinforcers or punishers, you can manage your students' future responses. And because you can manage your students' future responses, you can predict what they will be. Once you have learned about the role of consequences in the instructional cycle, you will know how to predict and manage your students' behavior.

Reinforcers

> A reinforcer is any event that maintains or increases the future probability of the response it follows.

If an event is to be a reinforcer, it must be something the student likes and for which he will behave or respond. Thus, reinforcing consequences are determined by the student's behavior, even though they may not seem like something positive or pleasant as far as you are concerned. To determine whether or not a consequence is reinforcing, you should note whether or not the student finds it pleasant and ultimately whether the response it follows increases in the future. If the response increases in the future, the consequence is a reinforcer. For example, consider a mobile hanging above a crib-bound student's head. When the student reaches and touches the mobile, it turns. If the student continues to reach and touch the mobile, it's very likely that the turning mobile is a reinforcing consequence. (Discovering reinforcers for your students will be covered in the next chapter.)

Practice Set 2D
Place a check mark beside each of the following situations in which a reinforcing consequence occurred.

_____ 1. Patrice walked to the teacher's desk and found a box of crackers. She ate 16 of them before her teacher walked up and took the box away. Patrice began to cry and regurgitated the crackers.

_____ 2. Sammy picked up puzzle pieces from the table and put them in his mouth. He looked around to see if one of the aides was watching him. Discovering that no one was looking at him, he spit out the puzzle pieces and put them back on the table.

_____ 3. Mary ate all the food on her plate. Mary's mother told her she was a good girl and gave her a piece of chocolate pie for dessert. Mary likes chocolate pie a great deal and ate the pie with gusto. After eating the pie, Mary gave her mother the sign for *eat*.

_____ 4. Ms. McMorrow, the physical therapist, was teaching Jerry to walk with crutches. Jerry took five steps and Ms. McMorrow gave him a drink of his favorite soda pop. After swallowing the soda pop, Jerry immediately took five more steps.

The answers are on page 189.

Punishers

A punisher is any event that decreases the future probability of the response it follows.

If an event is to be a punisher, it must be something the student does not like which decreases his responding. As was true of reinforcers, the selection of punishers must be based on the student's behavior, even though the punishers may not seem to you to be unpleasant events. To determine whether or not a consequence is punishing, you should note whether or not the student finds it unpleasant and ultimately whether the response it follows decreases in the future. If the response decreases in the future, the consequence is a punisher.

Practice Set 2E

Place a check mark beside each of the following situations in which a punishing consequence occurred. Consider each situation from the standpoint of what most students would find punishing.

_____ 1. On Monday Ann dipped her hand into a jar of paste and began eating it. Her teacher, Ms. Baker, told her to stop and spit the paste out. Ann responded by swallowing and then grabbing more paste. Ms. Baker walked over to Ann, told her that it was wrong to eat paste, and then gently brushed Ann's teeth with Listerine. Ann cried throughout the toothbrushing. Ms. Baker used the Listerine each time Ann attempted to eat paste. At the end of the week, Ann had not attempted to eat paste on either Thursday or Friday.

_____ 2. During the past 2 weeks, Patrick had been spitting at the other students an average of five times per day. This week his teacher, Ms. Brookes, had Patrick apologize to each person he spit at. Her records for the week show that Patrick has been spitting an average of eight times per day.

_____ 3. James tore the wheels off a toy truck. His instructor, Mr. Brown, took the truck away from James and put it out of sight. James began to cry and threw himself on the floor. A week later Mr. Brown gave James another truck. James played with the truck and did not attempt to tear the wheels off. A month has now gone by and James has shown no inclination to pull the wheels off his new toy truck.

_____ 4. Denise wouldn't share her toys and began to tantrum and scream when other students tried to play with her, so her teacher allowed her to play alone, since he figured that Denise would later decide to share. Three days have passed and Denise has made no attempt to share. She appears to be quite content playing by herself.

Answers are found on pages 189 and 190.

THE USE OF THE INSTRUCTIONAL CYCLE

We will now examine how you can use the three elements in the instructional cycle—the stimulus, response, and consequence—to instruct your students effectively.

To summarize, the *stimulus* is any physical object or occurrence in the environment that may set the occasion for a response to occur. A stimulus can be happenings, instructions, objects, or people. The *response* is the activity or behavior the student performs in the presence of the stimulus. The *consequence* is what happens to the student after the response.

Now let's look at how the instructional cycle can be used to help you instruct your students. Assume that you want to teach a student named Jim to "pull his T-shirt down from under his shoulders when instructed to do so." The response you want Jim to make is "pulling his T-shirt down from under his shoulders." To help him do this, you must provide a stimulus for this response. You decide to use three stimuli simultaneously: putting Jim's T-shirt on so that it is under his shoulders, positioning his hands so that they are on the bottom of the T-shirt, and giving the verbal instruction "Jim, shirt down." When Jim responds and pulls his T-shirt down to his waist, you'll want to give him a reinforcing consequence. Accordingly, you'll praise Jim—"Good, shirt down, Jim"—and give him a hug and a bite of graham cracker. Actually, you'll be giving Jim three reinforcers: praise, a hug, and a bite of cracker. (You know that these consequences will reinforce Jim's behavior because he has responded for them in the past.) If you use reinforcing consequences each time Jim pulls his T-shirt down when instructed, your training records will soon indicate that Jim's pulling his T-shirt down from his shoulders has greatly increased.

Whenever you want to teach a new behavior or increase an existing one, you must:

1. Determine exactly the response (behavioral objective) you want the student to make.
2. Choose a stimulus or stimuli that will serve as a cue(s) for the student to respond.
3. Select a reinforcing consequence(s) to increase the probability that the desired response will occur again.

Practice Set 2F

Read each of the following objectives and write the response the student should make and the stimulus or stimuli you would select to serve as a cue for that response. Also write a sentence to indicate why you presume that the consequence you have selected will strengthen the response, e.g., "Sally loves animal crackers" when the reinforcing consequence is a bite of an animal cracker.

1. Sally will turn the dial on the surprise busy box when instructed to do so.

    Stimulus: _____

    Response: _____

    Reinforcing Consequence: _____

2. Jeffrey will pull his pants up from the hip.

    Stimulus: _____

    Response: _____

    Reinforcing Consequence: _____

3. Beverly will brush the front surface of her teeth.

    Stimulus: _____

    Response: _____

    Reinforcing Consequence: _____

4. Richard will wheel his wheelchair 6 feet.

    Stimulus: _____

    Response: _____

    Reinforcing Consequence: _____

5. Reed will drink from a two-handled cup.

Stimulus: _____

Response: _____

Reinforcing Consequence: _____

Answers are found on pages 190 and 191.

You should make careful observations during any training or teaching situation so that you can pinpoint any problems in the instructional cycle. Observing the response provides information concerning the effectiveness of the stimulus. For example, if Jim couldn't pull his T-shirt down from his shoulders because the T-shirt was too tight, then the stimulus should be changed, e.g., Jim could be given a bigger T-shirt. Similarly, if Jim didn't respond to the verbal instruction alone, then a gesture by the instructor, such as pointing to the T-shirt and lowering her hand, could accompany the verbal instruction "Jim, shirt down."

Observing the response also provides information regarding the choice of the behavioral objective. For instance, an objective that is too easy or too difficult may have been selected. It may be too difficult for Jim to pull his shirt down without some physical guidance of his hands by the instructor. If this occurs, the instructor can simply select another objective that is more appropriate, e.g., "Jim will pull his T-shirt down from his shoulders when instructed to do so and with physical guidance of his hands provided by the instructor."

Sometimes the stimulus and response are appropriate, yet the student doesn't appear to be progressing. He may respond correctly on some days and incorrectly on others. If this occurs, the consequence is probably not very reinforcing, and another reinforcing consequence should be substituted for or added to the original reinforcing consequence. For example, if you have been using praise and a sip of juice with limited success, you could try substituting a piece of cookie for the juice or a hug as an additional reinforcing consequence.

Remember, observing the response and the effect of the reinforcing consequence helps you pinpoint problems in the instructional cycle. Most importantly, you need to collect accurate, reliable records of how the student is progressing. These records will tell you how successful the program is and whether or not you need to redesign it. (How to collect accurate records will be covered in Chapters 11 and 12.)

SUMMARY

The instructional cycle includes a stimulus, a response, and a consequence. The stimulus is any physical object or occurrence in the environment that may set the occasion for the response to occur. In effect, the stimulus serves to cue the response. The response is the behavior or activity the student performs in the presence of the stimulus. Finally, the consequence is what happens to the student after the response occurs. It may occur naturally or be arranged by others in the environment.

There are two main types of consequences: reinforcing consequences and punishing consequences. Reinforcing consequences increase the response they follow. They are called reinforcers because they strengthen the response and maintain or increase the probability that it will occur in the future. The relation between the response and reinforcer is called reinforcement. Punishing consequences decrease the response they follow. They are called punishers because they weaken the response and decrease the probability that it will occur in the future. The relation between the response and punisher is called punishment. Thus, we say that behavior is a function of its consequences.

Whenever you teach a new behavior or increase an existing one, you must (1) determine exactly the response (behavioral objective) you want the student to make, (2) choose a stimulus or stimuli that will serve as a cue(s) for the student to respond, and (3) select a reinforcing consequence(s) to increase the probability that the desired response will occur again. You can pinpoint any problems in the instructional cycle by making careful observations of the response and the effects the reinforcing consequence has on the response. Most importantly, you need to collect accurate, reliable records on student progress. These records will tell you whether or not you need to change the training program.

SUGGESTED READINGS

Graziano, A. M. (Ed.). *Behavior therapy with children* (2 vols.). Chicago: Aldine-Atherton, 1971, 1975.

Kazdin, A. E. *Behavior modification in applied settings.* Homewood, Ill.: Dorsey Press, 1975.

Lovaas, I. O., & Bucher, B. D. (Eds.). *Perspectives in behavior modification with deviant children.* Englewood Cliffs, N.J.: Prentice-Hall, 1974.

Reese, E. P. *The analysis of the human operant behavior.* Dubuque, Iowa: William C. Brown, 1966.

Thompson, T., & Grabowski, J. (Eds.). *Behavior modification of the mentally retarded.* New York: Oxford University Press, 1972.

Review Set 2

1. The instructional cycle is comprised of a s_____, r_____, and c_____.
2. A s_____ is any physical object or occurrence in the environment that may set the occasion for the response to occur.
3. A r_____ is the behavior the student performs in the presence of the stimulus.
4. The c_____ is what happens to the student after the response occurs.
5. There are two main types of consequences: r_____ ones and p_____ ones.
6. R_____ consequences increase the response they follow.
7. A r_____ is any event that maintains or increases the probability of the response it follows.
8. The relation between the response and reinforcer is called r_____.
9. P_____ consequences decrease the response they follow.
10. A p_____ is any event that decreases the probability of the response it follows.
11. The relation between the response and punisher is called p_____.
12. When teaching a new behavior or increasing an existing one, you must determine the r_____ you want the student to make, choose a s_____ to serve as a cue, and select a r_____ consequence.
13. If the c_____ isn't reinforcing, the student won't progress.
14. Observing the r_____ and the effect of the r_____ consequence helps to pinpoint problems in the instructional cycle.

Answers are found on page 191.

CHAPTER 3

Reinforcers

A reinforcer is the third element in the three-term contingency or instructional cycle. As discussed in the previous chapter, a reinforcer is an event that increases the probability that the response it follows will occur again. In effect, a reinforcer is something that students like and for which they will respond. It's crucial that you discover as many reinforcers as possible for each of your students because you can't increase behaviors unless you have a variety of reinforcers at your disposal.

Discovering reinforcers for severely and profoundly retarded students can be an arduous and sometimes difficult task. Unlike normal individuals, they often have very few reinforcers. There are two reasons for this. First, their learning deficits may have prevented them from engaging in a variety of potentially reinforcing activities. Second, they may not have been exposed to many potential reinforcers.

This chapter will show you how to overcome these problems by using the three main types of reinforcers for severely and profoundly retarded students. (These reinforcers also can be used with higher functioning students.) The concepts of satiation and deprivation will be explained to help you maximize the effectiveness of the reinforcers you choose. You'll also learn five ways to discover reinforcers for your students.

TYPES OF REINFORCERS

The three main types of reinforcers that are used for severely and profoundly retarded students are:

1. Edible reinforcers
2. Sensory reinforcers
3. Social reinforcers

There are some other types of reinforcers that you will learn about in later chapters, but these three are typically the most useful for strengthening desired behaviors.

Edible Reinforcers

> Edible reinforcers are the foods preferred by the student.

Edible reinforcers are the foods the student enjoys eating and for which she will respond. They are often the most powerful of the three types of reinforcers because everyone must have food in order to survive. Since your students are accustomed to edible reinforcers, you should use them when you begin teaching a new behavior or begin working with a new student. However, you should learn how to increase the variety of edibles the student will work for and eventually how to switch the student to other types of reinforcers (to be discussed shortly).

There are two kinds of edible reinforcers: solids and liquids. You can choose to use one, a combination of both, or switch back and forth from one to the other. For example, if you are using potato chips as a reinforcer during a teaching session, you may decide also to use cola or another type of liquid reinforcer later in the session. In this case, your decision would be based on the biological fact that after someone has been eating potato chips for a while she probably will become thirsty, and a liquid reinforcer therefore is likely to become very effective for a while.

Whichever kind(s) of edible reinforcer you choose to use, *you should provide a large variety*. Otherwise, the student will quickly tire of the same old fare and stop responding. For example, a student may work for Cocoa Puffs or squirts of lemonade for a few hours, but soon will tire of these foods if they are used all day, every day. When the student stops working or responding for an edible, we know that it's no longer reinforcing. This phenomenon is called *satiation*, and we say that the student is satiated on that particular edible. Satiation usually occurs after the student has been given the same reinforcer repeatedly. It doesn't matter what the reinforcer is; repeated exposure to it will usually result in the student being satiated.

> Satiation is the state that occurs when a reinforcer has been presented to the point that it is no longer effective in increasing or maintaining a behavior.

You should have no difficulty remembering to avoid the problem of satiation if you consider what it would be like to be given nothing to eat each day but hot dogs. How long do you think it would take before you couldn't stand the sight of another hot dog? Fortunately, satiation is normally a temporary state and the reinforcer should be effective again in the future, provided that you stopped using it for a while.

Remember, always provide a variety of edible reinforcers for your students, and when a student no longer responds or works for a particular edible, satiation has occurred and that edible is no longer reinforcing. When this happens, discontinue using that edible for a while. You'll know that the edible is again reinforcing when the student eagerly accepts it. The edible will again become reinforcing because of *deprivation.*

> Deprivation is the state that occurs when a reinforcer has been withheld until it once again is effective in increasing or maintaining a behavior.

Providing a variety of edible reinforcers permits you to take advantage of the effects of deprivation and avoid the problem of satiation because it's more likely then that the student will be in a state of deprivation for one or more of the reinforcers. As a result, she will be more likely to keep responding or working in the training or teaching environment. Deprivation, just like satiation, is a temporary state or condition, and the two are opposites. Deprivation ends when satiation occurs, and when the satiation effect wanes, deprivation begins to occur.

To sum up, maximize the chances that deprivation will exist and minimize the chances that satiation will occur. Besides using a variety of edible reinforcers, be sure to always deliver very small bits of each reinforcer. For example, an M & M can be broken into four parts so that one M & M can be used to reinforce four times. Using small bits will also reduce the possibility that your students will gain weight, have dental problems, or ruin their appetites for their regular meals.

It's also better to give small edible reinforcers for the simple fact that they don't take much time to consume. Foods that are long-lasting, such as gum, or that need preparation, such as unpeeled fruit or unshelled peanuts, take time away from instruction and may distract the student from the task. The following list of edibles is a sample of the wide number of solids and liquids that may be reinforcers for your students.

Liquids	Solids
Grape juice	Presweetened cereal (e.g., Froot Loops)
Orange juice	Popcorn
Apple juice	Potato chips
Milk	Corn chips
Water	Cookies
Kool-Aid	Raisins
Lemonade	Pretzels
Orangeade	Fruits (e.g., grapes)
Colas	Vegetable slices (e.g., carrot sticks)
Cocoa	Candy (e.g., M & Ms)
Tea	Mini-marshmallows
Decaffeinated coffee (for older students)	Peanuts (or other nuts)
	Cheese (e.g., cubes or pieces)

Edible and all other types of reinforcers should be given immediately following the correct or appropriate response. This is to make sure that (1) the connection between the desired response and the reinforcer is made, and that (2) other behaviors occurring between the response and reinforcer are not mistakenly reinforced.

To ensure that you can deliver edibles immediately, you should wear an apron whenever you are with your students. The apron should have multiple pockets to accommodate the variety of edibles you will be using. Liquid reinforcers can be placed in squirt bottles, such as catsup dispensers, that will fit easily into the apron pockets. Squirt bottles allow you to deliver a squirt of liquid without having the tip of the bottle touch the student's lips. In this way you can use the liquid reinforcer for several students without hygiene problems. To minimize the chances of satiation, at least two different types of liquids should be available at all times.

There are three potential problems associated with the use of aprons. The first is that some students may reach into the pockets if you aren't looking and grab the solid reinforcers. To prevent this problem, line each pocket with Velcro tape so that it remains closed until you wish to open it. The second problem is that certain edible reinforcers may melt, be crushed, wilt, or become sticky in the pockets. Such edibles would include fruit and vegetable slices, candies, marshmallows, raisins, pretzels, presweetened cereals, and potato chips. To solve this problem, place the edibles in a plastic bag (such as those used for sandwiches) and place the bag in the apron pocket. The third problem is that some male staff members may object to wearing an apron. To solve this problem, furnish them with carpenter's aprons. What the apron looks like is unimportant, as long as it serves its intended function.

Remember, all staff members *must* be wearing an apron that contains several pockets filled with squirt bottles of liquid reinforcers and a variety of solid edible reinforcers. This will ensure that reinforcers can be delivered immediately.

You should be aware of two points of caution regarding edibles that contain sugar. First, before using them, check the student's records to make sure she isn't diabetic. If she is, use artificially sweetened or dietetic edibles. (Be sure to clear their use with the student's physician.) Second, don't overuse edibles containing sugar, since excessive use can contribute to dental problems.

Sensory Reinforcers

> Sensory reinforcers are sensations that the student likes or enjoys.

Our senses play an important role in determining our reinforcer preferences. Most individuals, including severely retarded students, like pleasant sensations that involve sights, sounds, smells, and touch. There are five kinds of sensory reinforcers:

1. Tactile reinforcers
2. Vibratory reinforcers
3. Olfactory reinforcers
4. Visual reinforcers
5. Auditory reinforcers

A tactile reinforcer is any type of skin-to-skin contact between you and the student for which the student will respond. A tactile reinforcer can be a touch, a hug, a caress on the cheek, or a rub or massage in an appropriate area such as the student's back or neck. As you undoubtedly know, most students find such physical contact to be very reinforcing.

Vibratory stimulation also can be a powerful reinforcer, especially for multiply handicapped students. To deliver vibratory stimulation, briefly apply a vibrator to the student's neck, arms, hands, or legs. The duration of vibration should be anywhere between 15 and 30 seconds. The vibrator should be battery operated and carried in an apron pocket together with the edible and liquid reinforcers.

While vibratory stimulation can be a powerful reinforcer, it may not be appropriate for a few of your students. Some students are tactilely defensive, which means that they intensely dislike being touched either physically or with a vibrator. If you have such a student, you are probably already aware of the problem. To work on the problem of tactile defensiveness, try a shaping program (see Chapter 6) in order to gradually adapt the student to physical contact and vibratory stimulation. If you decide to embark on such a program, it's a good idea to enlist the aid of your facility's physical or occupational therapist, especially at the beginning.

A more serious problem can occur with some multiply handicapped students who suffer from cerebral palsy. *Under no circumstances should you use a vibrator with such students until they have been examined by a physical therapist and you have been given permission to use vibration.* Otherwise you run the risk of possibly causing a student some physical harm. There's no problem, however, if you simply wish to use your touch as a reinforcer with these students.

Olfactory reinforcers are pleasant-smelling substances. A good example would be the odors in a scratch-and-sniff book. Visual reinforcers are pleasant sights such as a spinning color wheel, a turning mobile, or a strobe light, while auditory reinforcers are pleasant sounds. Music is potentially a very powerful reinforcer to use with your students.

Social Reinforcers

> Social reinforcers are smiles, praise, attention, or friendly remarks that the student likes or enjoys.

The third and most important type of reinforcer is social reinforcers. Social reinforcers are a large part of everyone's life. We praise each other, smile at each other, and nod our heads or wave at each other; in short, we give some indication to others that we are pleased with them or that we like them. There is simply no question that praise or attention from someone important to us is very desirable and that we will work hard to obtain it.

Yet we were not born with a desire or need for social reinforcers. Rather we learned over time to enjoy praise, attention, and all the various social reinforcers. As infants we received edible and sensory reinforcers from our parents and we eventually paired our parents and their attention with these reinforcing events. (There also may be some biological and developmental bases for the development of social reinforcers in people, but such discussion is beyond the scope of this book.) Over time, our parents' attention became, in most cases, more important than the very basic reinforcers that we enjoyed as infants. Later we learned that praise had power, and that often it not only led to pleasant social interactions with people, but to other powerful reinforcers as well, such as money, prestige, or sex. Perhaps most importantly, we learned that the praise and attention from others made us feel better about ourselves because it increased our self-esteem.

Because food is basic and sustains life, some of your students may initially find edibles more reinforcing than praise. However, if they are to learn that praise is a powerful reinforcer and thereby progress toward normalization, you *must* deliver praise or some form of social reinforcer each and every time an edible or sensory reinforcer is given. This pairing will take your students through some of the same types of experiences that made social reinforcers important for you. The rule then is to *always pair a social reinforcer, normally praise, with the delivery of any reinforcer.* An example of how this pairing should be done follows.

Ms. Daniels is teaching Barry to take off his T-shirt. After Barry removes the shirt, Ms. Daniels immediately squirts grape juice into Barry's mouth and says, "Good, Barry, good taking off your shirt." Ms. Daniels knows how to reinforce; she paired the edible reinforcer (grape juice) with the social reinforcer of praise ("Good, Barry"). Furthermore, she used descriptive praise since she described the behavior she was praising. It's very important that you provide descriptive praise so that the student has an additional source of feedback on the performance of the appropriate behavior.

By pairing your praise with the delivery of edible reinforcers, your students will eventually begin to behave appropriately just for your praise. It is crucial that you use such pairing to develop a positive relationship with your students. You can't expect a student who doesn't know you, or who has had infrequent or frequent nonreinforcing interactions with you in the past, to find you very reinforcing until you've established a pattern and history of reinforcing her.

Your role as a reinforcer is especially crucial when it comes to the social reinforcer of attention. If you don't deliver attention for a student's positive behaviors, that student may seek your attention through negative or inappropriate behaviors. In fact, attention appears to be the one form of social reinforcement that becomes desirable to students very early in their lives, so much so that attention maintains a wide variety of inappropriate behaviors. Furthermore, social reinforcers are the one type of reinforcer that you can be sure will be delivered to the student outside the classroom or facility. Your task is to ensure that the student has a history of receiving social reinforcers for appropriate behaviors rather than inappropriate ones. Remember, *you are, or can be, an extremely powerful social reinforcer for your students,* and you should learn to think of yourself as such. It might help if you think of yourself as a big M & M. You always have a smile, a glance, and a soft word with you, and they do not cost anything, cause cavities, contain calories, or require an apron.

Practice Set 3A

Answer each of the following questions.

1. Mr. Boston was training Rita, a deaf student, to point to a picture of a toilet. During the 10:00 to 10:15 a.m. training session he asked Rita to point to a picture of a toilet and she did so 9 times out of 10. Each time Rita made the correct response, Mr. Boston reinforced her with a piece of a pretzel. At 10:16 a.m. Mr. Robertson began training Rita to wheel her wheelchair 10 feet forward. Rita responded correctly during her first trial, and Mr. Robertson reinforced her with a pretzel. At 10:17 a.m. Mr. Robertson again signed to Rita to move her wheelchair forward. Rita did not move the wheelchair but rather pointed at the water fountain and cried.

   a. Were pieces of pretzel a reinforcer for Rita at 10:00 a.m.? at 10:16 a.m.?

   b. Was the piece of pretzel a reinforcer for Rita at 10:17 a.m.?

   c. What would have been a good reinforcer for Rita at 10:17 a.m.?

2. Ms. Elliott, the physical therapist, had decided to teach Barbara to use a saddle walker. Ms. Elliot had never worked with her before. She believed that a good reinforcer for Barbara would be to say "Good" each time Barbara stood in the walker. When the training began, Ms. Elliot placed Barbara in the walker and each time Barbara's feet touched the floor, Ms. Elliot said, "Good." After 3 days, Barbara had not stood in the walker, but rather had merely touched her feet to the floor in a random fashion.

   a. What type of potential reinforcer was Ms. Elliot using?

   b. Is there another type of reinforcer that should have been used with or instead of the reinforcer "Good"?

   c. What would you have done to reinforce Barbara if it had been the first time you had ever worked with her?

3. Ms. Quigley was training Bart, a cerebral palsied child, to attend to visual stimuli. She held up a spoon and said, "Bart,

look." Each time Bart looked at the spoon, Ms. Quigley reinforced him by lightly caressing his cheek for 5 seconds.

    a. What type of reinforcer was Ms. Quigley using?

    b. Should Ms. Quigley have consulted a physical therapist before she touched Bart?

    c. Suppose Ms. Quigley had decided to use a vibrator to reinforce Bart's looking at the spoon. Should she have consulted a physical therapist before using the vibrator?

Answers are found on pages 191 and 192.

SPECIFIC REINFORCERS

Now that you've learned about the three main types of reinforcers, it's important to learn how to discover reinforcers for your students. Because an event is not a reinforcer for someone until it's been shown to increase his behavior, we can never simply say that chocolate candy, for instance, is a reinforcer for a particular student, although we know that, in general, most students like chocolate candy. Thus, it remains for us to give that student a piece of chocolate candy following one of his behaviors, and then to observe whether or not that behavior occurs again when it's followed by the candy. (Before using any potential edible or liquid reinforcer with a student, always check his medical records to ensure that he's not allergic to it.) If so, then we've established that chocolate candy is indeed a reinforcer for that student.

You can avoid a lot of problems by not assuming what will be reinforcing to a student. Rather regard anything that you would normally consider to be a reinforcer as only a *potential* reinforcer until it's been shown to increase a behavior. Once a reinforcer has been established and is being used, you should periodically determine whether or not it's continuing to be a reinforcer because a student's reinforcer preferences will change over time.

Remember, each student is unique and has a unique set of reinforcers that has been established by his learning history. One of your tasks as an instructor is to discover, establish, and increase each student's reinforcers.

There are five ways to discover a student's reinforcers:

1. Ask the student.
2. Observe the student.
3. Observe similar types of students.
4. Use the Premack Principle.
5. Use reinforcer sampling.

The first way to discover reinforcers for students is to ask them. This is the simplest way of determining what is reinforcing for students who have language. Your questions might be "What would you like?" "What would make you happy?" or "What can I do to make you happy?" Most verbal students will appreciate the opportunity to pick their reinforcers and will tell you what they would like. Yet it is amazing how often instructors fail to ask their students about their reinforcers. This simple effort on your part can save a lot of time and trouble.

Many of your students, however, will be nonverbal, so they won't be able to say what is reinforcing for them. And some verbal students may not be sure of what their reinforcers are. However, these students can still tell us what is reinforcing for them through a second way of discovering reinforcers.

The second way to discover reinforcers for students is to observe them. How do the students spend their time? Confucius said that if you watch someone, you will know him. Perhaps Confucius was the first behaviorist, because behaviorally oriented persons say that if you observe someone's behavior, you will know his reinforcers. The behaviors your students perform are those that they find reinforcing or which lead to a reinforcer. For example, if a student sits and rocks all day, we can say with assurance that either rocking is a reinforcer or leads to some reinforcer we can't see or measure. Similarly, it would be fairly safe to say that a student whose frequent misbehavior is followed by staff attention finds that attention reinforcing. So, if you observe your students, you'll learn what their reinforcers are.

Occasionally you'll observe a severely or profoundly retarded student who displays so few behaviors that it's difficult to determine what is reinforcing for him. In this situation, you could try the third way to discover a reinforcer. (You could also try reinforcer sampling, which will be discussed shortly.)

The third way to discover reinforcers for students is to observe students with similar backgrounds. Because severely retarded students often share similar deficits, experiences, and backgrounds, due to living in institutions or nursing homes, they often have similar learning histories in terms of the ways they behave and the kinds of reinforcers that have been available to them. As a result, you can learn a lot about a student by observing other students who are similar to him. What do other severely and profoundly retarded students on the living unit like to do? What do they find reinforcing? What do they spend their free time doing? The answers to these questions will suggest potential reinforcers for the student who doesn't appear to have any. After observing these similar students, make a list of their reinforcers to try as potential reinforcers for the student in question. You may have to try several of these potential reinforcers before you find one that is reinforcing.

A fourth way to discover reinforcers for students is to use the Premack Principle. The Premack Principle (which is named for David Premack) suggests that a behavior a student performs frequently can be used to reinforce a behavior he seldom performs. If the seldom performed behavior increases in frequency (occurs more often) when it's followed by the frequently performed behavior, then you've discovered a reinforcer. For example, Jimmy loves to flip a piece of paper with his fingers. Each day when Jimmy comes to school, he takes his jacket off, throws it on the floor, and rushes around to find a piece of paper to flip. Jimmy's teacher would like him to hang his jacket up when he comes in the classroom; however, Jimmy rarely if ever does so. Having just learned about the Premack Principle, Jimmy's teacher decides to try it. She tells Jimmy, "You must hang up your jacket before you can flip." To her surprise and delight, Jimmy dutifully begins to hang his jacket up every day. Jimmy's teacher has successfully used the Premack Principle: she has taken a behavior Jimmy frequently performs, flipping paper, and used it to reinforce hanging up his jacket, a behavior he seldom performs.

Jimmy's mother has the same problem with him. Each day when he comes home from school, he removes his jacket, throws it on the floor, and rushes around searching for a piece of paper to flip. One day she says, "You can flip paper now, but then you have to hang up your jacket." Do you think Jimmy will hang up his jacket when he finishes paper flipping? Probably not. The reinforcer, or high probability behavior of flipping paper, has already been delivered and therefore Jimmy's mother can't use it as a reinforcer for Jimmy to hang up his jacket. She did not use the Premack Principle correctly.

Remember, when using the Premack Principle, *always use the high probability behavior, the behavior that is performed frequently, to reinforce the low probability behavior, the behavior that is performed infrequently.* If the preferred behavior is to serve as a reinforcer, *it must follow the less preferred behavior.*

Perhaps you've encountered a student who can't tell you what he wants as a reinforcer and you can't find any particular reinforcer preferences during your classroom observations. He doesn't respond to the reinforcers of similar types of students and he doesn't perform any one behavior frequently enough for you to use the Premack Principle. For such a student you would use a reinforcer sampling procedure.

The fifth way of discovering reinforcers for students is reinforcer sampling. In this procedure you have the student try a variety of potential reinforcers. Thus, reinforcer sampling offers you an opportunity to determine whether or not the student will like the potential reinforcer. In essence, you're saying to the student, "Try it, maybe you'll like it."

If you recall some of your own experiences, you'll realize that many of your current reinforcers were established through reinforcer sampling. For example, some of us have had the experience of dining with a friend who says, "Why don't you try one of my raw oysters? Really, they're quite good, especially with some tabasco sauce and a little fresh lemon juice squeezed on them." You say, "Ugh, I couldn't possibly think of eating one of those slimy things." "Oh, just try one," your friend replies. "No, I couldn't." Your friend urges you again: "Aw, go on, just try one." You try one and find, to your surprise, that raw oysters really are quite good. In fact, you immediately decide to order a half dozen for yourself. You may not have been aware of it at the time, but you had just demonstrated the effectiveness of reinforcer sampling.

Reinforcer sampling is a very powerful way of discovering and establishing reinforcers. In fact, it's probably the most effective and useful of the five ways of discovering reinforcers. Reinforcer sampling is especially helpful in working with severely and profoundly retarded students who haven't had a lot of exposure to a wide variety of potential reinforcers. By using reinforcer sampling, you'll be expanding the number of reinforcers that can be used to motivate your students to learn.

Practice Set 3B

Answer each of the following questions.

1. Don is an 18-year-old mildly retarded student who attends a work activity center. He is verbal and engages in a variety of activities at the center. His instructor would like to discover some new reinforcers for him. What would be the most expedient method of determining some new reinforcers for Don?

2. Mr. Douglas wanted to discover reinforcers for Clare, a multiply handicapped, nonverbal student. He observed Clare for 5 days and discovered that she sat in a relaxation chair and did next to nothing. Since observing Clare didn't prove to be an effective method of determining a reinforcer for her, what method should Mr. Douglas try next?

3. William enjoys continually rocking whenever possible. His instructor, Ms. George, would like to teach William to hand her an object when requested to do so. Currently William will only occasionally hand her an object when asked. How could

Ms. George use the Premack Principle to teach William to hand her objects?

Answers are found on page 192.

SUMMARY

It's often difficult to find many reinforcers for severely and profoundly retarded students. The three main types of reinforcers commonly used with them are (1) edible reinforcers, (2) sensory reinforcers, and (3) social reinforcers.

Of the three types, edible reinforcers are often the most powerful and should be used when beginning work on a new behavior or with a new student. Edible reinforcers are the foods preferred by a student. They can be either solid or liquid. Overuse of any one reinforcer will lead to satiation, when the reinforcer becomes ineffective. It then must be withheld until deprivation occurs and it once again becomes reinforcing. A large variety of edibles should be available to maximize deprivation and minimize satiation for any one reinforcer. All instructors should wear aprons with pockets containing a number of reinforcers so reinforcement can be given immediately at any time.

Sensory reinforcers are sensations that the student likes or enjoys. There are five kinds: (1) tactile, (2) vibratory, (3) olfactory, (4) visual, and (5) auditory. Tactile reinforcers are any type of skin-to-skin contact. Vibratory reinforcers are contacts with a vibrator on the neck, arms, hands, or legs. Vibratory stimulation can be dangerous to students who have cerebral palsy, so permission from their physical therapist is needed before this form of reinforcement can be used. Olfactory, visual, and auditory reinforcers are smells, sights, and sounds that are appealing to students.

Social reinforcers are praise, smiles, attention, or friendly remarks that the student likes or enjoys. They are the most important type of reinforcer because the everyday world operates on the principle of social reinforcement. To make sure that students learn that praise is reinforcing, all reinforcers should be paired with a social reinforcer. Social reinforcers should be paired with edibles for initial instruction with a new student; but once the instructor becomes a social reinforcer for the student, the use of edibles should be reudced or eliminated.

An event is not a reinforcer for a student until that event increases one of the student's behaviors. Until this is shown, the event should be regarded as only a potential reinforcer. Potential reinforcers for students can be discovered in five ways: (1) ask the student, (2) observe the student, (3) observe similar types of students, (4) use the Premack Principle, and (5) use reinforcer sampling.

When working with a verbal student, the most expedient way to discover a reinforcer is simply to ask the student what he likes. If the student is nonverbal, you should observe him and make a list of activities, toys, or foods that he enjoys. If a student doesn't demonstrate reinforcer preferences in any areas, you should observe similar kinds of students, try reinforcer sampling by introducing the student to various types of potential reinforcers, or use the Premack Principle in which you use a behavior a student frequently performs to reinforce a behavior the student seldom performs.

Each student has different reinforcer preferences and these vary from minute to minute, hour to hour, day to day, and week to week. Effective use of reinforcers requires a variety of reinforcers, immediate reinforcement, and regular determination of each student's reinforcer preferences. Without effective reinforcers, students will not be motivated to learn.

SUGGESTED READINGS

Bailey, J., & Meyerson, L. Vibration as a reinforcer with a profoundly retarded child. *Journal of Applied Behavior Analysis*, 1969, *2*, 135-137.

Bijou, S. W. A functional analysis of retarded development. In N. R. Ellis (Ed.), *International review of research in mental retardation* (Vol. 1). New York: Academic Press, 1966.

Bijou, S. W., & Sturges, P. T. Positive reinforcers for experimental studies with children—consumables and manipulatables. *Child Development*, 1959, *30*, 151-170.

Gardner, W. I. *Behavior modification in mental retardation: The education and rehabilitation of the mentally retarded adolescent and adult.* Chicago: Aldine-Atherton, 1971.

Rynders, J. E., & Friedlander, B. Z. Preferences in institutionalized severely retarded children for selected visual stimulus material presented as operant reinforcement. *American Journal of Mental Deficiency*, 1972, *76*, 568-573.

Review Set 3

1. E_____ reinforcers are the foods a student prefers.
2. There are two types of e_____ reinforcers: solids and l_____.
3. S_____ occurs when a reinforcer has been presented to the point that it is no longer effective in increasing or maintaining a behavior.

4. D_____ occurs when a reinforcer has been withheld for a long enough period that it is once again effective in increasing or maintaining a behavior.

5. When using edible reinforcers, each instructor should wear an a_____ so that the reinforcers can be delivered immediately.

6. Reinforcers must be delivered i_____ if they are to be effective.

7. The five types of sensory reinforcers are t_____, v_____, visual, a_____, and o_____.

8. An example of a s_____ reinforcer is vibration applied to the student's neck, arms, hands, or legs.

9. A p_____ t_____ should be consulted before a vibrator is used with cerebral palsied students.

10. S_____ reinforcers include praise, smiles, attention, and friendly remarks.

11. Delivery of any reinforcer should be p_____ with a social reinforcer.

12. A p_____ reinforcer is an event thought to be reinforcing that has not yet increased a specific behavior.

13. The first way to discover a reinforcer for a verbal student is to a_____ him.

14. If you o_____ a student's behavior, you'll know what his reinforcers are.

15. Occasionally you'll observe a student who displays few behaviors. If this occurs, you should observe s_____ kinds of students.

16. The P_____ P_____ states that a behavior the student performs frequently can be used to reinforce a behavior the student seldom performs.

17. R_____ s_____ is a method whereby the student tries potential reinforcers.

18. Group the following reinforcers according to their type: edible, sensory, or social. (Hint: Two of them may be more than one type of reinforcer.)

A hug	A glance
M & M	Rubbing the student's feet with your hand
Vibration to the student's neck	Popcorn
Stroking the student's face with your hand	A nod

Kool-Aid	Milk
Bouncing the student on your knee	A back rub
Water	A Strauss waltz
A kiss	A spinning top
A smile	The odor of peppermint

Edible   Sensory   Social

Answers are found on pages 192 and 193.

CHAPTER 4

Structuring the Learning Environment

From the previous chapters, you now know how to use the instructional cycle to teach the students in your classroom. In this chapter, you'll learn how to structure your classroom or instructional area to produce effective behavioral increases. We'll consider three main points: creating as much of a distraction-free structured learning environment as possible, permitting the student to adapt to this environment, and then using noncontingent reinforcement before programming begins.

CREATING A DISTRACTION-FREE LEARNING ENVIRONMENT

Retarded students, especially the severely and profoundly retarded, are easily distracted and this distractability can cause difficulties when you attempt to teach them a new behavior. To provide the optimum learning environment, you must structure the environment so that you, the student, and the teaching materials are the only objects (stimuli) in the area. Anything that might create a distraction must be eliminated.

Elimination of Physical Distractions

Students are different and you will find that various students are distracted by different things. Some common distractions are extraneous noises, bright colors, toys or equipment other than those the student is working with, other students or instructors, and especially new adults.

To minimize or eliminate the many and varied distractions in your classroom, use an empty room that is devoid of distractions or create an area in your classroom or instructional area that is as

free of distraction as possible. If you aren't fortunate enough to
have a special training room, a distraction-free area can be created
by sectioning off a portion of a room with a screen or partition. It
is best to use a corner of the room. If you use a screen or a partition, make sure that the student faces the corner with her back to
the classroom. Regardless of how you choose to separate this area
from the rest of the room, it should (1) have no windows, or if it
does, curtains should be used to cover them, (2) have nothing on the
walls, (3) contain only the materials needed for instruction, (4) be
as far away from other students and instructors as possible, and (5)
be as far away from extraneous noises as possible.

The One-to-One Instructional Model

The appropriate learning environment for initial instruction of
severely and profoundly retarded students is a one-to-one instructional situation with only the student and a teacher or aide present.
For example, if a classroom contained 12 students, 1 teacher, and 2
aides, 2 staff members could be teaching one-to-one in 2 separate
distraction-free areas. The other staff member could watch over
the remaining 10 students as they played with toys or classroom
materials, and walk around and frequently reinforce any student
who was either playing appropriately or simply not misbehaving.
The toys and materials available in this general play area would be
changed daily. As each child finished her one-to-one session, her instructor would return her to the classroom area. The instructor
would then take another student to the one-to-one learning environment. Rotating the students through this one-to-one instruction would ensure that each student received the maximum quality
instruction possible. Generally, each one-to-one session would last
approximately 10 to 15 minutes.

The exception is when a complex behavior such as toileting or
self-feeding is being taught. For example, a toileting training program the author developed lasts from 6 to 8 hours each day until
the student can successfully toilet herself. During this period,
other students either receive one-to-one instruction (as described
before) if sufficient staff are available, or are watched and inter-
acted with in the manner previously described for a group.

The learning materials used in the one-to-one sessions can be
transported with the student or kept in a box or cabinet behind
the instructor's chair. The only materials in the student's view
should be those that will be used in the instructional session.
Those students who aren't involved in one-to-one instruction
should receive as much stimulation and as many activities as

possible while they wait for their one-to-one instruction. Because the emphasis here is on stimulating the students, a variety of interesting stimuli are not only permissible, but highly desirable.

From this brief description of the classroom or instructional setting, it's apparent that initially grouping severely and profoundly retarded students around a table for instruction, as is commonly done, is certainly not advocated. Doing so creates a chaotic situation where students look at each other, rather than at the instructional materials, and perform a variety of inappropriate behaviors to entertain each other or obtain attention from the instructors. In such situations the instructors spend much of their time simply preventing students from misbehaving, keeping students in their chairs, and awaiting the end of the workday. To avoid this situation, the one-to-one instructional model is used until the students are sufficiently prepared to be taught in a group setting.

It is difficult to say when a student is ready for group instruction since students progress at different rates. The best way to tell is to introduce the student to the group and see how she behaves. In the case of very low functioning students, group instruction may not be possible until the student will sit quietly at a table without bothering her neighbors and will attend to a task in front of her. In addition, these students will always require some individual instruction each day, especially if they are taught a complex skill such as toileting or dressing. For students who have difficulty sitting near others, it may be necessary to institute a shaping program (see Chapter 6) in which the student is gradually introduced to group instruction.

Practice Set 4A

Answer each of the following questions.

1. A classroom for severely and profoundly retarded students is devoid of any toys or pictures on the walls. Is this classroom an appropriate environment for the one-to-one instructional model? Yes or No

2. The following diagrams are of classrooms for severely and profoundly retarded students. Which classroom is an example of the one-to-one instructional model?

     • = student
    A = aide or paraprofessional
    T = teacher
    ⌒ = partition
    🚗= toys/equipment

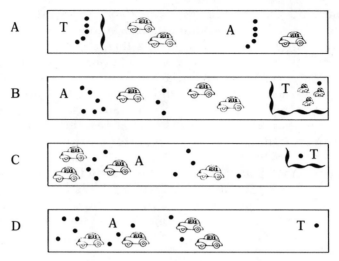

3. The following diagrams are of classrooms for severely and profoundly retarded students. Which classroom is an example of the one-to-one instructional model?

    • = student
    A = aide or paraprofessional
    T = teacher
    ～ = partition
    🚗🚗 = toys/equipment

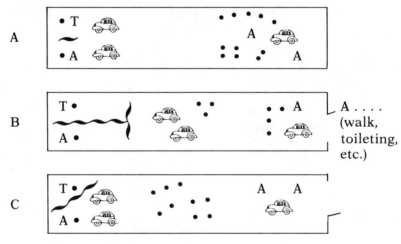

    D   None of the above

The answers are on pages 193 and 194.

PERMITTING ADAPTATION TO THE
LEARNING ENVIRONMENT

How do you behave when you enter a room filled with people you don't know? You probably remain silent and listen to the various conversations. However, after a period of time, you may join in one of them. When you bring a new puppy home, how does it behave during the first few days? It may hide under the furniture and whine until it begins to explore its new environment, but after a few hours it will be romping about the house. If a student is transferred to a new school in mid-year, what behavior does he exhibit in the classroom? He will probably watch other students for a while and then gradually join them in various activities.

Feeling comfortable in a new situation is important because we must adapt to new environments before we'll begin to behave either appropriately or inappropriately. Retarded students are no different. They must have the opportunity to explore any new environment or situation before they're expected to pay attention and learn. Once you create as much of a distraction-free structured learning environment as possible, give the student the opportunity to adapt to this new situation before you begin teaching him. By arranging for a student to spend some time in the learning situation before you begin your instruction, you'll be allowing him to adapt to this new environment.

If you don't permit the student to adapt, he may be distracted by some of the stimuli in the new environment and all your initial instructional efforts will be frustrated. Usually the adaptation process can be accomplished in less than half an hour. It's especially important that autistic students be given the opportunity to adapt. The following example illustrates the importance of allowing students to adapt to the teaching/training situation.

Mr. Johnson had begun toilet training Doug that morning. Doug was sitting on a toilet that contained a plastic bowl that would make a buzzing sound when Doug urinated in it. When the buzzer sounded, Mr. Johnson intended to reinforce Doug for having urinated in the toilet. The first time Doug urinated, the sound of the buzzer startled him. He reacted by ceasing to urinate, beginning to cry, and then jumping off the toilet and running around the room. Mr. Johnson immediately suspended the training and began sounding the buzzer repeatedly, independent of any of Doug's behavior. Within a matter of minutes, Doug demonstrated that he had adapted to the sound of the buzzer because he no longer acted startled whenever it sounded. At this point, Mr. Johnson resumed the toilet training program.

Remember, you should never begin instruction until the student has adapted to the new learning environment. You will know he's adapted to a new environment or situation when he begins to display the same behaviors that he displayed in his old environment. Thus, the student's behavior will tell you when he's adapted enough to the new learning situation to permit you to begin instruction.

Practice Set 4B

Answer each of the following questions.

1. William, a nonambulatory student, is habit or time trained and has successfully used a portable potty in his classroom for 6 months. William's instructor would like to teach him to urinate in the toilet located in a bathroom across the hall. How can the instructor help William adapt to the new environment?

2. Ruth is a 10-year-old profoundly retarded child. In order to learn how to walk, she needs to wear a leg brace. How could Ruth be helped to adapt to the leg brace?

3. Jeffrey arrived in your classroom today. He's lived in an institution for 8 of his 9 years and has been in a foster home for 1 month. Today, you're instructing your students in self-help skills. How can you help Jeffrey adapt to his new environment?

4. Today is your first day at your new job as an aide on an institution ward for profoundly retarded students. You walk into a room of 12 students and one other aide. How will you adapt to your new environment?

5. Today you plan to begin one-to-one eye contact training for Jason behind a partition located in a corner of the classroom. How will you help Jason adapt to this new situation?

The answers are on page 194.

USING NONCONTINGENT REINFORCEMENT

Noncontingent reinforcement is reinforcement that is not related to any specific response.

Before you begin programming, you must first establish yourself and the instructional area as reinforcing. You'll want to raise the density of reinforcement to accomplish this. To do so, use noncontingent reinforcement for a few days before you begin trying to increase behavior, for example, during the first week of the new school year and/or with any new students. Noncontingent reinforcement can occur often and at any time since it's not related to the students' behavior. It's simply the presentation of positive, pleasurable events. For example, during the first week of school, every student in Mr. Crane's room receives milk and cookies at 11:00 a.m. Mr. Crane is using noncontingent reinforcement because *everyone* receives milk and cookies regardless of their behavior at 11:00 a.m.

Mr. Crane used noncontingent reinforcement during the first week of school because he wanted the classroom and himself to acquire reinforcing properties for his students. (He and the classroom are paired with the presentation of the reinforcing events.) Mr. Crane knows that students must find him and the classroom reinforcing before they will be motivated to perform the behaviors he attempts to teach them. The use of noncontingent reinforcement also will help to reduce the students' inappropriate behaviors because they will be less motivated to misbehave for attention.

Practice Set 4C

Place a check mark beside each of the following situations that demonstrates the use of noncontingent reinforcement.

_____ 1. Mr. Kal passed out lollipops to all children who were on the gym mat.

_____ 2. Ms. White gave each student a pretzel stick as he got off the bus.

_____ 3. Mr. Thomas reads to Earl for 10 minutes every night at 8:00.

_____ 4. After Brian hung up his jacket, Ms. Gwynn pushed him on the swing.

_____ 5. Ms. Morgan gave lemonade to each child who was sitting quietly.

Answers are found on page 194.

The use of noncontingent reinforcement is not limited to the classroom. Think of times in your own life when reinforcers were delivered noncontingently or independent of your behavior. When new fast-food restaurants open, they often offer a free hamburger and fries, or a new miniature golf course may offer one free game of golf. These establishments are encouraging you to frequent their facilities by offering noncontingent reinforcement. (In effect, they're using a procedure very similar to reinforcer sampling. See Chapter 3.) Once you've sampled their facility and have been reinforced, they then begin to charge you for their goods or use of their facilities; use of the goods or access to the facilities becomes contingent on your purchasing behavior.

Another example of the initial use of noncontingent reinforcement to "hook" someone on the available reinforcers is courtship. During courtship, reinforcing compliments are often delivered noncontingently by your suitor. Often you don't have to display any specific behaviors to receive these adulations; you simply receive them because you are you. However, once the courtship ends in marriage, your spouse's reinforcing compliments generally become dependent on your specific behaviors. Your hair has to look extraordinarily nice for you to receive a compliment, or you may have to lose 10 pounds before you are told that you are handsome or pretty. Prior to marriage you received these compliments regardless of your hairstyle or how much you weighed. In effect, noncontingent reinforcement was used by your suitor to get you "hooked" on him or her as a major source of reinforcement. In the process of being "hooked" you fell in love with this source of reinforcement and ultimately married the person.

You'll use noncontingent reinforcement to "hook" your students in the same way. When you deliver social and edible reinforcers independent of any behavior, your students will pair you with the reinforcers you deliver, thereby establishing you as a reinforcer. (Be careful, however, not to give noncontingent reinforcement when the student is misbehaving; otherwise you may reinforce the misbehavior.) Once you become associated with reinforcement (usually after a few days), you'll dispense with all forms of noncontingent reinforcement and thereafter require specific appropriate forms of behavior before you reinforce.

SUMMARY

Retarded students are easily distracted, and this may cause problems when instruction is attempted. Thus, before instruction can begin, teaching locations should be created that are as free of distracting stimuli as possible. Initial teaching should consist of one-to-one instruction with only the student and instructor present, and group instruction should occur only after suitable training.

Once a distraction-free environment has been established, students should be given time to adapt to the new environment. A student has adapted to a new environment when she begins to display behaviors that were common for her to display in her old environments. When the student has adapted, instruction can take place.

In the first few days of the new school year and/or when a new student begins instruction, noncontingent reinforcement should be used. Noncontingent reinforcement is reinforcement not related to any specific response. This will establish the instructor and the instructional area as reinforcing and, once this occurs, reinforcement of only appropriate behaviors can begin.

SUGGESTED READINGS

Gambrill, E. D. (Ed.). *Behavior modification: Handbook of assessment, intervention and evaluation.* San Francisco: Jossey-Bass, 1977.

Gardner, W. I. *Behavior modification in mental retardation: The education and rehabilitation of the mentally retarded adolescent and adult.* Chicago: Aldine-Atherton, 1971.

Thompson, T. I., & Grabowski, J. (Eds.). *Behavior modification of the mentally retarded.* New York: Oxford University Press, 1972.

Review Set 4

1. Retarded students are easily distracted; therefore, instruction should take place in a d_____-f_____ environment.
2. Creating a distraction-free environment for severely retarded students requires o_____-to-o_____ instruction.
3. Students must have an opportunity to a_____ to the learning environment before instruction begins.
4. N_____ reinforcement is not related to the behavior of the student who is reinforced.
5. N_____ reinforcement should be used when working with new students or at the beginning of the school year.
6. Students must find you r_____ if they are going to be motivated to perform the behaviors you wish to teach them.

The answers are on page 195.

CHAPTER 5

Schedules of Reinforcement

In Chapter 3, you learned how to control the consequence portion of the instructional cycle by reinforcement. Now you'll find out how to use reinforcement more precisely and effectively. In this chapter, you'll learn to distinguish between contingent and noncontingent reinforcement, and continuous and intermittent reinforcement. We'll then consider four intermittent reinforcement schedules and how they can be used best with your students.

In the preceding chapter we defined noncontingent reinforcement as reinforcement that's not related to any specific behavior. Now let's consider contingent reinforcement.

CONTINGENT REINFORCEMENT

> Contingent reinforcement is reinforcement that depends upon a specific response.

Contingent reinforcement is the opposite of noncontingent reinforcement, since it is given only following a specified response. For example, if Ms. Brooks gives crackers to all her students at snack time independent of their behavior (what they are doing), then she's delivering noncontingent reinforcement. Conversely, if Ms. Brooks gives crackers to all students who are seated and quiet at snack time, then she's delivering the reinforcers contingent or dependent on the students' behavior of being seated and quiet. Thus, only those students who are in their seats and quiet will receive crackers.

Our everyday behaviors are strengthened and maintained in the same way; that's why we enjoy repeating the things we do well. We're reinforced when we do things well, and this reinforce-

51

ment builds and maintains our interest. For instance, an accomplished tennis player who continues to improve and win matches is likely to continue playing the game. However, if she is a lousy bowler who can't seem to improve and has a poor average, she's likely to lose interest quickly and give up the sport. When we compare these two sports, it becomes obvious that a person will continue playing the sport for which reinforcement is received, while giving up the sport for which there is little, if any, reinforcement.

Contingent reinforcement also will strengthen the behaviors of severely and profoundly retarded students. Billy was a 14-year-old multiply handicapped boy who had lived in an institution for 12 of his 14 years. He now resides in a nursing home. The first behavior the instructional aide wanted Billy to perform was indicating when he had to use the toilet. Billy had no expressive language, but his receptive language was excellent, so the aide taught Billy to point to a picture of a toilet that was taped to the arm of his wheelchair. During the training of this behavior the aide approached Billy once an hour. Each time Billy signaled that he needed to use the toilet and then used the toilet, the instructor gave Billy a brief, 1-minute shoulder massage to maintain and strengthen the behavior. The reinforcer of receiving a shoulder massage was made contingent (dependent) on Billy's indicating his need to use the toilet, and then using the toilet. The aide's program worked. After a few days, Billy would reliably point to the picture of the toilet whenever he needed to use the toilet, in order to receive the massage.

In summary, to establish or strengthen a response, always use contingent reinforcement and reinforce the response each and every time it occurs. Over time the student will perform the desired response more often in order to receive more reinforcement, thereby strengthening and maintaining the desired response.

Practice Set 5A

Place a check mark beside each of the following situations that demonstrates the use of contingent reinforcement.

_____ 1. Mr. Smith gave each of his children 25 cents on Friday.

_____ 2. Mr. Smith gave 25 cents to each child who helped him clean the yard.

_____ 3. Each time a resident used the toilet, Ms. Johnson gave him 10 points.

_____ 4. A bag of potato chips was given to each child who walked to the bus.

_____ 5. After lunch, Popsicles were given out to all of the students.

Answers are found on page 195.

The effectiveness of your instructional program depends on the proper use of contingent reinforcement. Two types of contingent reinforcement you'll use with your students are *continuous* and *intermittent reinforcement.*

Continuous Reinforcement

> Continuous reinforcement is the reinforcement of every occurrence of a response.

Continuous reinforcement is used when you begin to teach a new response (behavior) because it strengthens a new or weak behavior better than any other schedule of reinforcement. A *schedule of reinforcement* is simply a description of when the reinforcer will be delivered. Thus, in a continuous schedule of reinforcement, the specified behavior is reinforced every time it occurs. For example, when teaching Sally eye contact, you'd use continuous reinforcement by saying, "Good, you looked at me," and giving Sally an edible reinforcer each and every time she looked at you.

> A schedule of reinforcement is a description of when a reinforcer will be delivered.

Continuous reinforcement is the only type of reinforcement schedule you should use when beginning to teach a new behavior. However, it isn't the schedule of reinforcement you should use to maintain a behavior once that behavior has been established. This is because behaviors reinforced on a continuous reinforcement schedule will disappear rapidly if the continuous reinforcement ceases. You've encountered this situation in your own life. For instance, turning on a light switch is a behavior that is typically reinforced every time you do it. If the light doesn't go on, you don't stand there flipping the switch; after a few flips, you give up and change the light bulb. Or how long do you continue to put money in a vending machine that doesn't work? Even if you've gotten a soda from the machine every day for a year, you stop placing coins in the machine very quickly once you've determined that it doesn't work.

When the reinforcement for a behavior ends, we say that the behavior is being *extinguished* and that the behavior is on extinc-

tion. *Extinction* simply means that there will be no more programmed reinforcement associated with the performance of the
behavior. Eventually the behavior will be extinguished, which
means that the person will no longer perform the behavior
because there's no longer any reinforcement for doing so.

In the previous examples, the behaviors of turning on a light
switch or putting coins in a vending machine quickly extinguished because they had been on a continuous schedule of reinforcement: we've come to expect lights and vending machines to
work (reinforce us) the first time we perform the behaviors
associated with them. Thus, extinction (where we no longer perform the response) takes place quickly. The rapid extinction of a
continuously reinforced behavior also occurs in the classroom.

Janice was 11 years old and had been tube fed all her life. Her
instructor was interested in teaching Janice to eat a liquid diet so
that she would no longer require tube feeding. When Janice first
began to eat the liquid diet, her instructor reinforced her with
"Good girl, Janice," and stroked her hand each time she swallowed a spoonful of liquid. Soon the instructor found that it was
taking Janice approximately an hour to eat each meal, in part
because of the continuous delivery of reinforcement after each
swallow of food. The instructor also had grown tired of reinforcing each of Janice's eating responses and had very little time to
spend with the other students during mealtime. Since Janice now
ate her liquid meals three times a day, her instructor decided to
stop all reinforcement. Within a day, Janice had stopped swallowing and was spitting out the liquid.

In this example we see the major disadvantage of continuous
reinforcement: when the reinforcement stops, the behavior stops.
Furthermore, it's quite unnatural to go through life reinforcing a
student for every single appropriate response and to do so would
result in very little progress in the student's overall behavior.
Since it's not realistic to continue to reinforce every appropriate
response and because there's always the danger that the behavior
will disappear if a few reinforcers are skipped, we must use
another type of reinforcement—intermittent reinforcement—to
maintain the student's newly learned behaviors. Intermittent
reinforcement will be discussed in the next section.

Practice Set 5B

Place a check mark beside each of the following situations that
demonstrates the use of continuous reinforcement.

_____ 1. Mr. Jacobs is teaching Samuel to put his dishes in the
          sink after he has finished eating. On Thursday, Samuel

put his dishes in the sink at breakfast, lunch, and dinner. Mr. Jacobs reinforced Samuel at lunch and dinner.

_____ 2. Sally was learning to take off her jacket. She took it off when she came into the classroom in the morning and her teacher gave her a cracker. When Sally took her jacket off after recess she was given a Tootsie Roll.

_____ 3. Ricky picked his clothes up off the floor and his mom let him stay up to watch television for an extra 30 minutes on Monday. On Tuesday, Ricky picked up his clothes and his dad took him for an ice cream cone.

_____ 4. Marilyn was learning to feed herself. The first week she fed herself at each meal and the aide took her for a walk outside after each meal. The second week Marilyn fed herself at each meal, but she was not taken for a walk on Tuesday and Thursday.

_____ 5. During physical therapy, Jacques was learning to sit up. Whenever Jacques sat up on the gym mat, his therapist gave him a squirt of Kool-Aid. Later that day, he sat up on a mat in the classroom and his teacher also gave him a drink of Kool-Aid.

The answers are on pages 195 and 196.

Intermittent Reinforcement

> Intermittent reinforcement is the reinforcement of some, but not all, occurrences of a response.

Many of your behaviors aren't reinforced each time they occur; they are only reinforced some of the time, that is, on an intermittent basis. You don't always get the party you dialed on the telephone, and turning on the radio doesn't always result in your hearing one of your favorite songs; yet you continue to use the phone and the radio. These behaviors don't disappear (extinguish) after one or two nonreinforced occurrences. In general, *the more intermittent the reinforcement, the more likely you are to persist in performing the behavior.* (Unless the reinforcer occurs too little, in which case, you may not listen to a radio station that rarely plays your favorite tunes.)

Once your student has learned a new behavior and has been on a schedule of continuous reinforcement, you'll be ready to use a schedule of intermittent reinforcement. Intermittent reinforcement does not follow *each* response; rather it follows only *some* responses.

The importance of changing from continuous to intermittent reinforcement cannot be overemphasized because the use of intermittent schedules eliminates five disadvantages associated with the use of continuous reinforcement. These are:

1. Continuous reinforcement can result in satiation. The student who is reinforced for every appropriate response soon becomes satiated on the reinforcer(s) and his performance will drop dramatically as a result. For example, a student who is continuously reinforced with edibles all morning long is hardly hungry in the afternoon and therefore will not be motivated to respond for edibles.

2. As discussed previously, when continuous reinforcement is used and then terminated abruptly, the behavior you're trying to maintain or strengthen will disappear rapidly, that is, extinguish quickly.

3. Having to provide continuous reinforcement "wears you out." It's simply not feasible to reinforce each and every response over a long period of time.

4. Continuous reinforcement uses up reinforcers very rapidly. This can be expensive if edible reinforcers are being used.

5. Using continuous reinforcement makes generalization more difficult to achieve because the student comes to expect to be reinforced each time he responds appropriately.

One way to avoid reinforcing every response is to deliver fewer reinforcers for the same number of responses. For instance, if you want to teach a student to hang up his jacket when he enters the classroom, begin by reinforcing him for hanging up his jacket every day. Then, when your records show the student will reliably hang up his jacket every day, say for a week, switch to intermittent reinforcement. To do so, simply reinforce the student for hanging up his jacket every other day, then every third day, etc. You will probably find that there will be no decrease in the behavior because the student will continue to hang his jacket up every day.

Let's return to Janice for a moment. Janice was tube fed for years and she's now on a liquid diet. She's on continuous reinforcement because she's reinforced with praise and stroking each time she swallows the liquid. However, it's become time consuming and tiring for the instructor to reinforce Janice continually, so she switches Janice to an intermittent schedule of reinforcement. Now Janice receives praise ("Good girl, Janice") and her hand is stroked after every two or three swallows rather than after each one. Eventually the instructor will spread out the delivery of these reinforcers to a point where Janice only needs to be reinforced after every 10th swallow. Thus, the use of an intermittent schedule saves the instructor time, allows her more time with the other students at mealtime, and starts Janice on the road to independent eating.

Remember, intermittent reinforcement should be used to maintain and strengthen the new behavior after you have first established it by using continuous reinforcement. The advantages of using intermittent reinforcement are:

1. It will not cause satiation problems.
2. The newly learned behavior will persist when the intermittent schedule is reduced. Thus, the behavior is more resistant to extinction.
3. Reinforcement agents, such as teachers, aides, and parents will not become worn out or bored.
4. The available supply of reinforcers can be portioned out. Using intermittent schedules is less expensive and this can be important when program budgets are tight.
5. Generalization of the behavior, where the behavior occurs in other situations or under different conditions (see Chapter 13), is more likely, since almost all "normal behaviors" are on intermittent reinforcement schedules.

Practice Set 5C

Place a check mark beside each of the following situations that demonstrates the use of intermittent reinforcement.

_____ 1. Each time Joshua looked at his teacher, she placed a spoonful of pudding in his mouth.

_____ 2. Barbara received a piece of candy bar after every fourth correct response when playing lotto.

_____ 3. Steven was playing in the sandbox. Every 5 minutes his mother told him he was a good boy for playing so nicely.

_____ 4. Each day when he returned from school, Nicholas was given a kiss by his mother.

_____ 5. Elizabeth cleaned her room every day for a week. She was reinforced with a soda on Tuesday, a quarter on Thursday, and a new magazine on Saturday.

Answers are found on page 196.

SPECIFIC SCHEDULES OF REINFORCEMENT

As mentioned previously, intermittent reinforcement is used to maintain and increase appropriate behaviors once they have been established through continuous reinforcement, and the specification as to which behaviors will be reinforced is called a schedule of reinforcement. There are two basic types of intermittent schedules of reinforcement. One, the *ratio schedule*, is based on the number of responses that are performed. Thus, ratio schedules are response dependent. The other, the *interval schedule*, is based upon the interval of time between reinforced responses. Thus, interval schedules are time dependent. The importance of understanding these schedules is that they determine many things about the behavior being reinforced: whether it will disappear rapidly or be persistent, whether it will occur at high rates or very slowly, and when it is likely to occur.

Ratio Schedules

When reinforcement is contingent upon a specified number of responses occurring before the reinforcer is given, the behavior or response is on a ratio schedule of reinforcement. There are two types of ratio schedules of reinforcement: *fixed ratio* (FR) and *variable ratio* (VR).

Fixed ratio schedules

> In a fixed ratio schedule, the reinforcer follows a predetermined number of responses.

A fixed ratio schedule is one in which a prespecified number of responses must occur before the response is reinforced. An example of a fixed ratio schedule in the everyday world is when factory workers are paid on the basis of how many units they complete. As an example of the use of fixed ratio schedules with retarded individuals, consider Sandra. If Sandra is reinforced with vibration after every three sips of a drink, then Sandra is on a fixed ratio three (FR 3) schedule. FR 3 indicates that every third response is to be contingently reinforced.

Another example of fixed ratio schedules is when Mr. Lott teaches two of his students, Stewart and Mike, to work a 16-piece puzzle. Mr. Lott gives Stewart a pat on the back and an edible each time he correctly places 4 of the 16 puzzle pieces. Thus, Stewart is on an FR 4 schedule of reinforcement. Mr. Lott gives Mike a pat and edible each time he correctly places 2 puzzle pieces. Thus, Mike is on an FR 2 schedule of reinforcement. Once Stewart successfully completes the puzzle on the FR 4 schedule twice, Mr. Lott will change the fixed ratio schedule so that Stewart must place 7 pieces correctly before he is reinforced. In effect, Mr. Lott will be requiring more responses (7 instead of 4) for the same amount of reinforcement. When Mike successfully completes the puzzle on the FR 2 schedule twice, Mr. Lott will change Mike's schedule from FR 2 to FR 4. Eventually Mr. Lott will require Stewart and Mike to work the entire 16-piece puzzle (FR 16) before they receive a reinforcer.

By now it may have occurred to you that a continuous reinforcement schedule is also an FR 1 schedule of reinforcement, since the predetermined number of responses is one.

Students on fixed ratio schedules usually respond in two characteristic ways. First, they tend to respond very rapidly until the number of responses needed for reinforcement is achieved. Second, they tend to pause or rest after they have received the reinforcer. Knowing about these characteristics is important because they illustrate two disadvantages of using a fixed ratio schedule:

1. A very high fixed ratio schedule, say, FR 50, can produce an exhausted and overworked student who will cease responding. (Remember, the student is likely to respond rapidly until the number of required responses is achieved.) As a result, you should keep the schedule reasonable.

2. The pause that occurs after the reinforcer is delivered can be a problem when you want the student to display a constant or steady rate of behavior. Constant behavior doesn't occur on fixed ratio schedules because the student stops for a while each time she is reinforced before beginning to respond again. The student knows that no additional reinforcement will be forthcoming until she again performs the specified number of responses.

The rules for using a fixed ratio schedule are to (1) determine the student's present level of performance and (2) initially select an easy ratio schedule that provides reinforcement after only a few responses and then gradually increase the number of responses required for reinforcement. The advantage of a fixed ratio schedule is that it's simple to use: you need only reinforce a fixed number of responses.

Practice Set 5D

Answer each of the following questions.

1. Jessica is on an FR 3 schedule for handing her teacher the

correct object in a two-choice discriminative task. When will
Jessica be reinforced?

2. Alfred, a student in a prevocational program, is on an FR 5
schedule for correctly placing yellow bolts in a box. When
will Alfred be reinforced?

3. Thomas puts three pegs in a pegboard and Ms. Brown reinforces him with a candy corn. He places three more pegs in
the board and is reinforced once again. Thomas is on an FR
_____ schedule.

4. Renee dries eight dishes and Mr. Owens tells her that she is
doing a good job. She dries eight more dishes and once again
Mr. Owens tells her that she is doing a good job. Renee is on
an FR_____ schedule.

Answers are found on page 196.

Variable ratio schedules

> In a variable ratio schedule, the reinforcer follows
> a different number of responses each time such
> that over time a specific average number of re-
> sponses is reinforced.

The other type of ratio schedule is the variable ratio schedule
in which the number of responses necessary to receive a reinforcer varies. As a result, the student can never predict how many
responses she must make before she'll be reinforced. This, of
course, is in contrast to the fixed ratio schedule, where the student can easily predict when she'll be reinforced since it's always
after the same number of responses. As a result it's best to switch
a student from a fixed ratio schedule to a variable ratio schedule
whenever possible.

There are many examples of the variable ratio schedule
operating in our lives. In fact, most events are variable, especially
those over which we have little direct control. For instance, people who gamble are on variable ratio schedules. They sometimes
win and sometimes lose but cannot predict when.

Now let's see how to determine and use a variable ratio schedule in the classroom. Remember Sandra, the student who received
vibration after every third sip of drink she took (FR 3)? Her instructor, Mr. Otis, would now like to use a variable ratio schedule to
reinforce Sandra's drinking. He decides to reinforce Sandra on a
variable ratio four (VR 4) schedule. Accordingly, he'll reinforce
Sandra after two sips, six sips, three sips, and five sips of a drink.
The reinforcement schedule is indeed variable, ranging from rein-

forcing after two to six sips, but Sandra is reinforced on the *average* of every fourth response (2 + 6 + 3 + 5 = 16 ÷ 4 = 4 responses on the average). Hence, we say Sandra is reinforced on a VR 4 schedule.

When using a variable ratio schedule, you must determine the ratio before instruction begins. For example, Mr. Bennett was teaching Harry to walk using a saddle walker. Mr. Bennett had reinforced Harry on an FR 6 schedule for several days. Harry had to take six steps in succession in order to receive a reinforcer. Then Mr. Bennett decided to reinforce Harry on a VR 6 schedule. Harry was to be reinforced on the average after every six steps he took. The first time Mr. Bennett used this schedule, he reinforced Harry for taking two steps, then reinforced Harry after five steps, then nine steps, six steps, and finally after eight steps. Harry took a total of 30 steps and was reinforced five times, or he was reinforced on the average of every six steps he took (VR 6).

The advantage of a variable ratio schedule is that the student can't predict when the reinforcer will be delivered, and therefore will usually not pause after receiving a reinforcer. As a result, a variable ratio schedule produces very steady patterns of behavior and is thus an excellent schedule for the long-term maintenance of a behavior or skill.

The disadvantages of using a variable ratio schedule are:

1. It's time consuming because you must determine the ratio schedule before using it.
2. It requires some expertise on your part. Accordingly, you probably shouldn't use this schedule until you have developed a reasonable level of expertise.

Practice Set 5E

Answer each of the following questions.

1. Grant is on a variable ratio schedule. He's putting together felt tip pens and is reinforced for three pens, then six pens, then four pens, and then three pens. He's on a VR _____ schedule.

2. Samantha is on a variable ratio schedule. Her house mother reinforces her for making beds. She's being reinforced for eight beds, then three beds, then seven beds, and then two beds. Samantha is on a VR _____ schedule.

3. Howard is learning to stack towels. Mr. Adams is reinforcing Howard on a VR 5 schedule. Give an example of how often Mr. Adams should reinforce Howard on the next five occasions that he stacks towels.

The answers are on page 196.

Interval Schedules

An interval schedule of reinforcement is based on the passage of time, that is, the interval between reinforced responses. In other words, the first response that occurs following an interval of time is reinforced. Thus, interval schedules are time-based schedules. There are two types of interval schedules of reinforcement: *fixed interval* (FI) and *variable interval* (VI).

Fixed interval schedules

> In a fixed interval schedule, the reinforcer follows the first prespecified response after a prespecified amount of time has elapsed.

In a fixed interval schedule, the first prespecified response is reinforced after a prespecified period of time has elapsed. Thus, on a fixed interval 1 minute (FI 1 minute) schedule, the first response that occurs after 1 minute has passed would be reinforced.

Fixed interval schedules occur very often in our lives. You may work on a fixed interval schedule such that you are paid every Friday, every other Friday, or once a month. You know that this fixed period of time must pass before you're reinforced by receiving your paycheck. Another example would be checking your mailbox. You have a good idea of what time the postman is likely to deliver the mail, so you don't even bother to check for mail until shortly before the postman normally arrives at your door. From that time on, you check your mailbox periodically until you find the mail.

For an example of the classroom use of fixed interval schedules, let's return to the drinking program for Sandra. We've trained Sandra to drink and now want to maintain and strengthen her drinking behaviors. To do so, we'll put Sandra on an FI 1 minute schedule of reinforcement. At the beginning of the meal, we'll set a timer to ring in 1 minute. After the timer rings, we'll reinforce Sandra with vibration (a vibrator placed on her arm for 5 seconds) and praise following the first prespecified drinking behavior that occurs, that is, taking a sip from her cup.

Let's look at a couple of other examples. Ms. Jamison is using an FI 30 second schedule to maintain Donald's on-task behavior. Every 30 seconds, Donald receives a reinforcer if he is on task. Ms. Jamison also is using a fixed interval schedule to strengthen and maintain Jenny's on-task behavior. Jenny had been on FI 10, FI 20, and FI 30 second schedules of reinforcement and currently is on an FI 40 second schedule. Ms. Jamison has gradually lengthened the intervals so that 40 seconds must now pass before Jenny receives reinforcement. Eventually Ms. Jamison can build up the FI schedule by carefully lengthening the intervals so that Jenny will receive a reinforcer for being on task after 5 minutes have elapsed. This point is very important. When using a fixed interval schedule, try to gradually lengthen the interval so that it is manageable, that is, long enough that you have time to work with other students during the interval. Be careful, however, not to set too long an FI interval when you first put a student on that schedule. Otherwise, the reinforcement may not come frequently enough for the student to continue responding.

The advantage of using a fixed interval schedule is that you don't have to count responses; rather, all you need to do is set a timer and then reinforce the first response that occurs after the timer rings. As a result, the fixed interval schedule is quite easy to use. However, there is a major disadvantage of using this schedule. Like fixed ratio schedules, fixed interval schedules do not produce steady rates of responding. The student gradually becomes accustomed to the interval and will pause after she is reinforced, thus delaying the performance of subsequent behaviors. For example, if Sandra were on an FI 2 minute schedule for drinking, she would quickly learn that after she received reinforcement, 2 minutes would elapse before that reinforcement was available again. Therefore, she could pause for almost 2 minutes before continuing to drink so long as she responded after the interval had elapsed. As you can see, a fixed interval schedule may not generate very many behaviors.

Practice Set 5F

Place a check mark beside each of the following situations that demonstrates the use of a fixed interval schedule of reinforcement.

_____ 1. Alex was given 10 points at the end of every 5 minutes if he was reading his history book.

_____ 2. Melissa was given a Froot Loop at the end of every 10 seconds if she was in her seat.

_____ 3. John received a bite of candy after he'd stacked six blocks.

_____ 4. Gregory was reinforced for every five milk cartons he placed on the shelf.

_____ 5. Marilyn received an M & M every 10 minutes if she was still playing in her backyard.

Answers are found on pages 196 and 197.

Variable interval schedules

> In a variable interval schedule, the reinforcer fol-
> lows the first prespecified response after different
> intervals of time have elapsed such that over time
> a specific average interval is maintained.

The second type of interval schedule is the variable interval
(VI) schedule of reinforcement in which the time requirement is
not held constant but rather is a specified average. The variable interval is the most desirable of all reinforcement schedules to use in
the classroom. The following example illustrates why.

Earlier we left Ms. Jamison using a fixed interval schedule of
reinforcement to reinforce the on-task behavior of two of her students. Although things had gone well for a few days, the major
disadvantage of the fixed interval schedule had emerged and was
causing problems. Both Donald and Jenny had quickly become
accustomed to the fixed intervals, and their on-task behaviors
had become sporadic because they were not on task until they
heard the timer ring. To solve this problem, Ms. Jamison decided
to use a variable interval schedule. She did so because she knew
that the students could not predict when reinforcement was
available on this schedule. In order to avoid missing a reinforcement opportunity, then, Donald and Jenny would have to respond
(be on task) more of the time. Ms. Jamison put Donald on a
variable interval 30 second (VI 30 second) schedule. During the
first on-task session, Donald was reinforced by Ms. Jamison saying, "Good working, Donald" after 10 seconds, 40 seconds, 25 sec-
onds, 20 seconds, 30 seconds, 35 seconds, 50 seconds, 20 seconds,
40 seconds, and 30 seconds. Thus, Donald was reinforced on a VI
30 second schedule or 10 times within a period of 5 minutes (300
÷ 10 = an average of 30 seconds). Whenever the timer rang,
regardless of the interval, Donald had to be on task in order to
receive the reinforcers. Donald continued to stay on task without
pausing because he never knew when the reinforcement would
occur. Thus, the variable interval schedule Ms. Jamison used produced a steady and constant rate of on-task behavior. As you
might guess, Ms. Jamison also implemented a variable interval
schedule for Jenny's on-task behavior.

The variable interval schedule is perfect for use in the classroom because you aren't tied to a timer or to counted responses. In
fact, it isn't even necessary in most cases to calculate the average
interval between reinforcers. Rather, all you must do is randomly
reinforce the student when you observe him performing the

desired behavior. Of course, in the beginning you would want to make the intervals short until the behavior achieved the constancy you desired. After that, you could merely reinforce randomly.

At this point you should know that a variable ratio schedule can be used in the same way. Randomly reinforcing a student who is performing a number of responses will allow you to take advantage of the effects of a variable ratio schedule without having to calculate the average number of responses that will be reinforced.

The variable interval schedule also permits you to control and reinforce the behavior of a large number of students. For example, you could keep all of your students in their seats if you did nothing more than randomly reinforce those who were seated and then stretched out the time between reinforcers.

Practice Set 5G

Place a check mark beside each of the following situations that demonstrates the use of a variable interval schedule of reinforcement, and answer the last question.

_____ 1. A teacher randomly gives happy face stickers to any student who is in his seat.

_____ 2. John receives a corn chip if he's still finger painting after 3 minutes have elapsed.

_____ 3. A child who is quietly playing in his room is periodically visited by his mother and praised for playing nicely.

_____ 4. Jose is reinforced after he picks up three toys, then five toys, and finally after he picks up four toys.

_____ 5. Susie receives an orange slice on a VI schedule if she's not rocking. The intervals after which she'll be reinforced for not rocking are 1 minute, 45 seconds, 2 minutes, 30 seconds, 15 seconds, 1 minute, and 20 seconds. Susie is on a VI _____ schedule.

The answers are on page 197.

There are two advantages of using variable interval schedules of reinforcement:

1. They produce rapid, constant behavior because, unlike fixed interval schedules, the student can't predict when the reinforcer will be available.

2. They are easy for you to use because they allow time to work with a group of students. For example, when the intervals are set for 10 or more minutes, you have time to attend to more than one student and still reinforce the student(s) who is on the variable interval schedule.

Variable interval schedules are common in our own lives. For example, the frequency with which you are praised by your boss, spouse, or friends normally occurs on a variable interval schedule. You're never quite sure when a compliment will be forthcoming. The letters you receive from a friend may arrive on a variable interval schedule. Or how often do you attend the movies? Is it once a week, twice a month, or an average of once a month? The variable interval schedule approximates the contingencies in the natural environment, more so than any other schedule. This, of course, is another reason it's such a good schedule to use because it helps program the student for normal contingencies or "normalization."

SUMMARY

Contingent reinforcement is the opposite of noncontingent reinforcement because it depends upon the occurrence of a specific response. Contingent reinforcement is used to strengthen and maintain the responses of your students. The two types of contingent reinforcement are continuous reinforcement and intermittent reinforcement.

Continuous reinforcement is used when you begin to teach a new behavior. Every response is reinforced. The disadvantages of continuous reinforcement are that (1) satiation can occur, (2) continuously reinforced behaviors are subject to rapid extinction when reinforcement ends, (3) realistically, not every response can be reinforced, (4) reinforcers are used up rapidly, and (5) generalization is difficult to achieve.

One way to avoid reinforcing every response is to deliver fewer reinforcers for the same number of responses. You can do this by using intermittent reinforcement, thereby reinforcing only some of the responses. The specification as to which behaviors will be reinforced is called a schedule of reinforcement.

There are two types of intermittent schedules of reinforcement: ratio schedules and interval schedules. A ratio schedule is based on the number of responses that must be performed to obtain reinforcement; it is response dependent. An interval schedule is based on the interval of time between reinforced responses; it is time dependent.

There are two types of ratio schedules: fixed ratio and variable ratio. In a fixed ratio schedule, the reinforcement follows the performance of a predetermined number of responses. Continuous reinforcement is a fixed ratio schedule; specifically, an FR 1. In a variable ratio schedule, the reinforcer follows a different number of responses each time, maintaining a specified average number of responses over time.

There are two types of interval schedules: fixed interval and variable interval. In a fixed interval schedule, you reinforce the first prespecified response that occurs after a prespecified amount of time has elapsed. In a variable interval schedule, variable intervals of time occur between reinforced behaviors, maintaining a specific average interval over time.

Fixed ratio schedules are easy to use, but must be planned with reasonable ratios to avoid exhausting students, and fixed interval schedules have the advantage of not requiring any counting. However, both types of fixed schedules produce responding that is followed by a pause, which in some cases can be lengthy. This is because the student can predict when the reinforcement will be delivered and thus will not respond over time at very high rates. Variable ratio schedules produce high rates of behavior, but they can be time consuming and require some expertise. Variable interval schedules are the easiest to use and are the most beneficial to your students. They produce steady rates of behavior without pauses because the student can't predict when reinforcement will be forthcoming, since it appears to be random. Also, you can use variable interval schedules to reinforce the behavior of a large group of students, since you are essentially presenting random contingent reinforcement. Thus, variable interval schedules are the most useful intermittent schedules for classroom use.

SUGGESTED READINGS

Bijou, S. W., & Orlando, R. Rapid development of multi-schedule performance with retarded children. In L. P. Ullman & L. Krasner (Eds.), *Case studies in behavior modification.* New York: Holt, Rinehart & Winston, 1965.

Orlando, R., & Bijou, S. W. Single and multiple schedules of reinforcement in developmentally retarded children. *Journal of the Experimental Analysis of Behavior,* 1960, *3,* 339-348.

Reese, E. P. *The analysis of the human operant behavior.* Dubuque, Iowa: William C. Brown, 1966.

Stephens, C., Pear, J. J., Wray, L. D., & Jackson, G. C. Some effects of reinforcement schedules in teaching picture names to retarded children. *Journal of Applied Behavior Analysis,* 1975, *8,* 435-447.

Review Set 5

1. N_____ reinforcement is not related to any specific behavior.

2. C_____ reinforcement is reinforcement that depends on a specific response.

3. C_____ reinforcement can strengthen or maintain a behavior.

4. There are two types of contingent reinforcement: (1) c_____ and (2) i_____.

5. C_____ reinforcement is when the behavior is reinforced each time it occurs.

6. C_____ reinforcement is the only type of reinforcement you should use when beginning to teach a new behavior.

7. A s_____ of reinforcement is a description of when a reinforcer will be delivered.

8. One of the disadvantages of continuous reinforcement is that the behavior e_____ rapidly when the reinforcement ceases.

9. Another disadvantage of continuous reinforcement is s_____ can occur.

10. Other disadvantages of continuous reinforcement are that it "w_____ you out," u_____ up reinforcers, and makes g_____ difficult.

11. I_____ reinforcement is when only some of the appropriate responses are reinforced.

12. One way to avoid reinforcing every response is to deliver fewer r_____ for the same number of responses.

13. After you have used continuous reinforcement to teach a new behavior, you should use i_____ reinforcement.

14. R_____ schedules are based on the number of responses that are performed. Therefore, they are r_____ dependent.

15. I_____ schedules are based on the interval of time between reinforced responses. Therefore, they are t_____ dependent.

16. When using a r_____ schedule of reinforcement, the reinforcer is contingent on a prespecified number of responses occurring before one response is reinforced.

17. The two types of ratio schedules are f_____ ratio and v_____ ratio.

18. A f_____ ratio schedule is one where a prespecified number of responses must occur before the response is reinforced.

19. Students on fixed ratio schedules usually respond very rapidly and then p_____ after they are reinforced.

20. During a v_____ r_____ schedule of reinforcement, the reinforcer follows a different number of responses each time.

21. The advantage of a variable ratio schedule is that it is not p_____. Thus, there is no pause after the reinforcer, and very steady patterns of responding are produced.

22. An i_____ schedule is based on the interval of time between reinforced responses.

23. In a f_____ i_____ schedule, the first response is reinforced that occurs after the passage of a fixed period of time.

24. Students on fixed interval reinforcement schedules do not perform many behaviors because they p_____ after the reinforcer is delivered and do not begin responding again until the next interval has almost elapsed.

25. In a v_____ i_____ schedule, a variable amount of time occurs between reinforced behaviors.

26. In a variable interval schedule, the student cannot p_____ when reinforcement will be available. Therefore, she will respond at a very constant rate.

27. With a v_____ i_____ schedule, it is possible to reinforce the behavior of a large group of students.

28. A variable interval schedule can be regarded as r_____ contingent reinforcement.

29. Probably the best reinforcement schedule to use in the classroom is the v_____ i_____ schedule.

Answers are found on pages 197 and 198.

CHAPTER 6

Shaping

Much of your time is spent teaching students new, functional behaviors. This process is enhanced by the use of reinforcement, as was discussed in the previous chapter. However, with retarded students, problems often arise because their physical and intellectual deficits have limited the range of appropriate behaviors available for reinforcement. It's difficult to raise their level of functioning by using reinforcement alone because you can't reinforce a behavior that doesn't occur. The teaching task then becomes one of creating completely new behaviors for your students. The technique for doing this is called *shaping*. This chapter will show you how to change the response section of the instructional cycle through shaping to reach instructional goals. You'll learn seven steps in the behavior shaping process, and four ways of maximizing the success of your shaping programs.

> Shaping is the reinforcement of successive approximations of a target behavior to produce a behavior that is currently not in the student's behavioral repertoire.

Shaping is used to increase the number of behaviors in a student's *behavioral repertoire*, the behaviors that a particular student, at a particular time, is capable of performing. We first select the *target* or *terminal behavior*, which is the desired behavior that does not occur but which we wish to establish. Then we select a behavior or response that the student does perform and that resembles the target behavior in some way. This behavior is called the *initial behavior*.

Shaping is then used. Once we have increased the frequency of the initial behavior through reinforcement, that behavior will

71

not be reinforced again until it more closely approximates the target behavior. We continue to require these "successive approximations" of the target behavior until the target behavior finally occurs. The reason shaping works so well is that the student must continue to change his behavior in the direction of the target behavior in order to receive the reinforcer.

Shaping is a very important part of everyone's life because it's used to teach us new skills. Just about every complex skill we've learned was acquired through a shaping procedure. For example, as young children we eventually learned to speak clearly because our parents selectively reinforced sounds that made sense, like "Mommy," and ignored nonsensical sounds, like "Bommy." The more clearly we spoke, the more reinforcing attention we received and the greater impact we had on our environment. As we entered school, we were taught to write through shaping. First we practiced by making a variety of marks on a page over several days. Next we traced dotted lines that vaguely resembled the letters of the alphabet but which meant nothing. After we were able to follow the dotted lines, we were required to link them together to form letters of the alphabet. When we became proficient printers of single letters, we were required to join some of them together to form words. Later, or in the next school year, we were taught cursive writing by first tracing dotted lines that curved and so forth until finally we could link cursive letters together. As adults, most of our complex skills were developed by shaping techniques, whether we were learning to play tennis, speak a foreign language, cook, drive a car, or master the behavioral principles in this book.

THE BEHAVIOR SHAPING PROCESS

Shaping is comprised of the following steps:

1. Select the target behavior.
2. Select the initial behavior that the student currently performs and that resembles the target behavior in some way.
3. Select powerful reinforcers with which to reinforce the initial behavior, the successive approximations of the target behavior, and the target behavior.
4. Reinforce the initial behavior until it occurs frequently.
5. Reinforce successive approximations of the target behavior each time they occur.
6. Reinforce the target behavior each time it occurs.

7. Reinforce the target behavior on an intermittent schedule of reinforcement.

There are some important factors to consider when you follow these steps so that you can avoid potential problems.

Selecting the target behavior. The target behavior must be specified precisely so that you'll know when the student has performed it and so that you reduce the chances of strengthening other irrelevant behaviors through reinforcement. (Strengthening irrelevant behaviors will only serve to prolong the shaping process.) Clear-cut criterion levels for success at each step or stage must be specified. An acceptable level of performance of the target behavior should also be specified so that you know when the behavior shaping process is complete. For example, suppose you wish to teach a student to eat independently with a spoon. The criterion level of acceptable performance of the target behavior might be that the student will feed herself independently with a spoon on 10 successive trials without spilling any food. A good behavioral objective (see Chapter 1) should be written to ensure correct identification of the behavior and its criterion level.

Selecting the initial behavior. The best way to determine the initial behavior to be reinforced is to observe the student in the natural or training setting for a few days before you begin shaping. By doing so, you should observe a behavior that resembles the target behavior enough to be used as the starting point in the shaping process.

Selecting a powerful reinforcer(s). The student's motivation to perform must be kept at a high level. Accordingly, select the most powerful reinforcers available to you (see Chapter 3). Bear in mind that we will be requiring the student to continuously change her behavior as she proceeds toward the target behavior. The use of powerful reinforcers will ensure that the student will be motivated to keep trying various approximations until she performs one that is reinforced.

Reinforcing the initial behavior until it occurs frequently. By reinforcing the initial behavior frequently, you will be increasing the chances that a slight variation of it will occur that is a closer approximation to the target behavior.

Reinforcing successive approximations of the target behavior. A good deal of skill is involved in knowing how long to reinforce one level of performance before requiring the next level. Shaping places increasing demands on the student and only your skill will ensure its success. For example, if you reinforce one level of performance (approximation) too long, that behavior will become so rigidly established that it will be very difficult to motivate the student to move on to the next performance level. On the other hand, the student's new behavior may extinguish if you attempt to make her progress too rapidly because she will not have had time to associate the new behavior with reinforcement. As a general rule of thumb, figure on reinforcing from three to five performances at a given level before moving to the next level. There's no simple way of learning how to decide when to require a higher level of performance, since this decision depends on the shaper's skill and knowledge of the student. And the only way to develop this skill is to conduct as many shaping programs as you can. In this way, *your skill as a behavior shaper will be shaped.*

Reinforcing the target behavior each time it occurs. Use continuous reinforcement to firmly establish the target behavior in the student's behavioral repertoire.

Reinforcing the target behavior on an intermittent reinforcement schedule. Once a target behavior is established, the use of intermittent reinforcement will ensure that it is maintained in the student's behavioral repertoire.

AN EXAMPLE OF THE SHAPING PROCESS

The following example illustrates the use of the seven steps to shape eye contact, the most rudimentary of skills. The development of eye contact is important because the student must learn to attend to you before he can be taught any other functional behaviors.

Target behavior. When requested to do so, Merle will maintain eye contact with the instructor for 2 consecutive seconds. Merle will have successfully achieved the criterion level for the target behavior when he gives eye contact for 2 seconds on at least 90% of all requested trials over 100 trials (i.e., Merle must respond correctly on at least 90 of 100 trials).

Initial behavior. The initial behavior will be Merle's orienting his head and eyes so that he is facing the instructor and their eyes make fleeting contact (a glance).

Reinforcers. Whenever Merle responds appropriately, he will be given an edible reinforcer (peanuts, his favorite food), a tactile reinforcer (a touch on his cheek), and a social reinforcer (praise), "Good looking at me, Merle." In order to be reinforced, all instances of eye contact must occur within 5 seconds of the instruction "Look at me."

Reinforcing the initial behavior. Merle's orienting of his head and glancing at the instructor will be reinforced until it reaches at least 90% of all requested trials over 50 trials (i.e., Merle must respond correctly on at least 45 of 50 trials).

Successive approximations of the target behavior.
Initial behavior—Glance
Successive approximation—Eye contact for 1 second
Target behavior—Eye contact for 2 seconds

Merle's successive approximation, 1 second of eye contact, will be reinforced until it reaches at least 90% of all requested trials over 50 trials.

Reinforcing the target behavior. Each instance of 2 seconds of eye contact will be reinforced until Merle achieves the 90% criterion level of eye contact on 100 trials. Thereafter, 2 seconds of eye contact will be reinforced intermittently until Merle responds at a 90% criterion level on an FR 5 schedule for 100 trials (i.e., Merle must give 2 seconds of eye contact on five consecutive trials before he receives a reinforcer). When this criterion is reached, a generalization program for eye contact will be implemented.

Now, let's see how Merle's eye contact would be shaped. Behind a partition in the corner of the classroom, the instructor and Merle are seated at a table facing each other. A bowl of peanuts is located to the instructor's right and out of Merle's reach. In front of the instructor is a recording sheet and a pencil. The instructor begins by taking a peanut out of the bowl and placing it in Merle's mouth. She does this several times until Merle's eyes track the peanut from the bowl to his mouth. The instructor is now ready to shape eye contact because Merle is intently tracking the peanut in her hand with his eyes. The next time she reaches for a peanut, she lifts the peanut to her eyes. As Merle's eyes follow the peanut to her eyes, she says, "Merle, look at me." As soon as his eyes meet hers, she quickly places the peanut in his mouth, strokes his cheek, and says, "Good looking at me, Merle." She then scores a correct response on her recording sheet.

Each eye contact shaping session consists of 20 trials and there are 100 trials each day. The use of five sessions throughout the day eliminates the possibility that Merle will become bored or satiated on peanuts (see Chapter 3).

Once Merle has glanced at the instructor 90% of the time or better over 50 trials, the instructor is ready to require Merle to maintain his eye contact for 1 second. Now, when his eyes make contact with hers, she counts to herself "a thousand and one." If Merle maintains eye contact during the second, she reinforces him in the manner already described.

Once Merle has given the instructor 1 second of eye contact on at least 90% of 50 requested trials, she is ready to begin reinforcing the target behavior of 2 seconds of eye contact. She conducts the eye contact shaping trial as she always has, with the exception that Merle must maintain eye contact with her for 2 seconds. When he does so, he is reinforced. When he fails to maintain eye contact for 2 seconds or does not respond within 5 seconds of the instruction (verbal prompts will be discussed in Chapter 7), she returns the peanut to the bowl and records an incorrect response on her recording sheet. The eye contact shaping program ends when Merle gives her 2 seconds of eye contact on at least 90 of 100 trials (90% eye contact or better).

At this point, the instructor is ready to begin reinforcing Merle's eye contact intermittently so that it will be maintained in his behavioral repertoire. Accordingly, she reinforces eye contact every other successful trial (FR 2), every third successful trial (FR 3), and finally after every fifth trial (FR 5). Once Merle gives her 2 seconds of eye contact on at least 90 of 100 trials on the FR 5 schedule, the instructor is ready to begin her generalization and maintenance program (see Chapter 13). Also, she must fade holding the peanut near her eyes (fading will be described in Chapter 7).

Practice Set 6

Answer the following questions.

1. There are seven steps in the behavior shaping process: (a) select a t_____ behavior, (b) select an i_____ behavior that the student currently performs, (c) select powerful r_____, (d) r_____ the initial behavior until it occurs frequently, (e) reinforce s_____ a_____ of the target behavior each time they occur, (f) r_____ the target behavior each time it occurs, and (g) once the target behavior has been performed several times, reinforce on an i_____ schedule of reinforcement. (Showing you the first letter of each correct response is an attempt to help shape your performance of the correct response.)

2. Ms. Wolf would like to use shaping to teach Laura to eat independently with a spoon. Currently Laura will grasp the spoon and scoop food but will not raise the spoon to her mouth. Ms. Wolf decides that the best way to use shaping would be to reinforce Laura for raising her spoon to her mouth. To do so, Ms. Wolf will apply a portable vibrator to Laura's right shoulder for 2 seconds and say, "Good eating, Laura." In the beginning, she will reinforce Laura for any slight upward

movement of the spoon towards the mouth. After that, Ms. Wolf will require Laura to move the spoon a little closer to her mouth each time in order to receive the vibration and praise. In this way Laura will have to perform more of the feeding action herself each time. Ms. Wolf believes that Laura will eventually feed herself once she has the spoon within an inch of her mouth. At that point, Ms. Wolf simply plans to reinforce each bite for a few trials and then discontinue the use of the vibrator. In this example:

   a. What is the target behavior?

   b. What is the initial behavior?

   c. What are the two reinforcers?

   d. How will Ms. Wolf ensure that the initial behavior occurs frequently?

   e. What are the successive approximations and how will they be reinforced?

   f. How will the target behavior be reinforced continuously?

   g. How will the target behavior be reinforced intermittently?

3. When using shaping, it's important to specify a c_____ level of success for the initial behavior, the successive approximations, and the target behavior.

4. The best way to determine the initial behavior to be reinforced is to o_____ the student in the natural or training setting for a few days prior to beginning the shaping program.

Answers are found on pages 198 and 199.

WAYS TO MAXIMIZE SUCCESSFUL SHAPING

There are several ways of maximizing the success of the shaping process. One way is to combine a discriminative stimulus with shaping. A *discriminative stimulus* is a stimulus that sets the occasion for the response to occur because it has been associated with reinforcement. In the eye contact training example, two discriminative stimuli were used to occasion the eye contact response. They were the peanut held near the instructor's eyes and the verbal instruction "Merle, look at me." It's hard to imagine an instance in which you wouldn't use a discriminative stimulus to facilitate the shaping process.

A second way to maximize the shaping process is to combine physical guidance (a physical prompt, as described in Chapter 7) with the shaping. In Chapter 7 you'll learn that all prompts are discriminative stimuli. In the previous example, the instructor could have used physical guidance to increase the likelihood of a correct eye contact response by gently guiding Merle's chin with her left hand so that his head was oriented toward hers. She would give this physical guidance at the same time she said, "Look at me."

A third way is to combine an imitative prompt with the shaping (modeling and imitation are covered in Chapter 8). An example of the use of an imitative prompt in shaping that is somewhat similar to shaping eye contact would be shaping speech. In that case, the instructor would hold the peanut next to her lips, say "Merle, say 'Mm,' " form her lips so that she could make the "Mm" sound, and then make the "Mm" sound. The instructor's formed lips and her "Mm" sound would both be examples of imitative prompts. A final way is to combine fading with shaping, which will be discussed in the next chapter.

Shaping is one of the most important and powerful techniques available for increasing appropriate behaviors. It requires great skill and this skill can only be acquired by doing as much shaping as you can and by keeping careful records of both your progress and the student's.

SUMMARY

Shaping, the reinforcement of successive approximations, is used to produce a behavior that is not in the student's behavioral repertoire. This new behavior is called the target behavior. The behavior shaping process includes seven steps: (1) selecting a target behavior, (2) selecting an initial behavior that the student currently performs and that resembles the target behavior in some way, (3) selecting powerful reinforcers, (4) reinforcing the initial behavior until it occurs frequently, (5) reinforcing successive approximations of the target behavior, (6) reinforcing the target behavior each time it occurs, and (7) reinforcing the target behavior on an intermittent schedule of reinforcement. The four ways of maximizing the success of the behavior shaping process are to (1) combine a discriminative stimulus with shaping, (2) combine physical guidance with shaping, (3) combine an imitative prompt with shaping, and (4) combine fading with shaping.

SUGGESTED READINGS

Bensberg, G. J., Colwell, C. N., & Cassell, R. H. Teaching the profoundly retarded self-help skills activities by behavior shaping techniques. *American Journal of Mental Deficiency*, 1965, *69*, 674-679.

Foxx, R. M., & Azrin, N. H. *Toilet training the retarded: A rapid program for day and nighttime independent toileting.* Champaign, Ill.: Research Press, 1973.

Garrard, K. R., & Saxon, S. A. Preparation of a disturbed deaf child for therapy: A case description in behavior shaping. *Journal of Speech and Hearing Disorders,* 1973, *38,* 502-509.

Horner, R. D. Establishing use of crutches by a mentally retarded spina bifida child. *Journal of Applied Behavior Analysis,* 1971, *4,* 183-190.

Review Set 6

1. S_____ is the reinforcement of successive approximations.

2. The goal of shaping is to develop a n_____ behavior that is not in the student's behavioral r_____.

3. The behavior you intend to establish through shaping is called the t_____ behavior.

4. You begin the shaping process by reinforcing a response or behavior that is currently in the student's repertoire. This response is called the i_____ behavior.

5. Shaping involves a gradual change in the r_____.

6. The shaping process can be maximized by (a) combining a d_____ stimulus with shaping, (b) combining physical g_____ with shaping, (c) combining an i_____ prompt with shaping, and (d) combining f_____ with shaping.

Answers are found on page 199.

CHAPTER 7

Prompting and Fading

In the previous chapter we overcame the problem of students not having various functional behaviors in their behavioral repertoires. This was done with shaping, a gradual change in the response portion of the instructional cycle. Now we turn to two other problems in teaching retarded students that can be overcome by changing the stimulus portion of the cycle. First, these students often need additional help or cues in order to perform the desired behaviors. *Prompting* is the technique used to provide these extra discriminative stimuli, or *prompts*. In this chapter we'll present the three types of prompts and show you how to use them. The other problem arises from the use of prompting. Students often become dependent on prompts and won't perform newly learned behaviors on their own. Rather, they'll wait for you to prompt them. In order to foster independence and decrease the student's reliance on us, we use a technique of eliminating prompts called *fading*. We'll describe ways to fade all three types of prompts. At the end, we'll also state three cardinal rules for prompting and fading.

PROMPTING

A prompt is an auxiliary discriminative stimulus that is presented to cue the student to perform a specified behavior.

As discussed earlier, a discriminative stimulus is a stimulus that sets the occasion for a behavior to occur because that stimulus has been associated with reinforcement. Thus, all behaviors that are reinforced are preceded by discriminative stimuli. It makes no difference whether the reinforcer is delivered by someone, such as an instructor giving a student a piece of candy, or by the environment, such as when the student opens a jar and takes a piece of candy. In either case, some type of discriminative stimulus sets the occasion for the reinforced response to occur. Discriminative stimuli can occasion either appropriate or inappropriate behavior, since either can be reinforced. For example, a plate of food can be a discriminative stimulus for the response of eating with a spoon or grabbing food.

The use of discriminative stimuli to cue the student to perform a particular appropriate behavior is called *prompting* and the discriminative stimuli themselves are called *prompts*. What differentiates prompts from other discriminative stimuli is that the prompt is delivered by someone (the instructor) for a specific purpose. Thus, a prompt is nothing more than a cue to the student that you want him to behave in a certain way and that this behavior will be followed by a reinforcer. We refer to a prompt as an auxiliary discriminative stimulus because it's given *in addition to* whatever natural discriminative stimuli are associated with the behavior. For example, if you wanted a student to pull up his pants, you might prompt him to do so by telling him "Pull up your pants," pointing to his pants, and guiding his hands in raising his pants. Your delivery of these prompts (discriminative stimuli) would be in addition to the natural discriminative stimuli for pants raising that were present such as you, the pants, and the particular location such as the bedroom where the training had been taking place. You would use the prompts to teach the student to raise his pants because the natural discriminative stimuli had not been sufficient in the past to set the occasion for pants raising.

The importance, then, of prompts is that they enable us to greatly increase the likelihood that a behavior will occur. Prompting is an especially valuable technique for teaching profoundly and severely retarded students because they have so few appropriate behaviors or skills. By incorporating prompting into training programs, we can greatly increase the students' acquisition of appropriate behaviors and complex sequences of behaviors.

Types of Prompts

There are three types of prompts: verbal, gestural, and physical. Verbal prompts are no more than a verbal instruction. The instruction "Merle, look at me" is a verbal prompt, as is any instruction that we give. For example, a teacher telling her aide to conduct an eye contact training session with Merle—"Sarah, take

Merle with you and work with him on eye contact"—is using a verbal prompt. A gestural prompt might include pointing, looking in a particular direction, or raising your hand. Two common gestural prompts that are understood by everyone are a policeman extending his arm with his palm facing you to indicate that you are to stop and someone placing her finger over her lips to indicate that you should be silent. Physical prompts involve actual physical contact with someone, for example, physically guiding a student to leave his chair and stand up.

How to Prompt

For high functioning students and normal individuals, it's only necessary to use prompting during the first few training trials. After that the individual usually understands what he is to do and does it. For low functioning students, however, it's often necessary to use prompting for many trials, especially when you are attempting to teach a complex sequence of behaviors. This presents a problem because the student can become dependent on the prompter (instructor) and the prompts. For instance, the student may stand in the bathroom with his pants around his knees waiting to be prompted to raise them. To overcome this problem, we fade the prompts as soon as possible (to be described shortly), so that the student will have to rely on his own initiative, motivation, and memory.

Prompts can range from very obvious, conspicuous events to very faint, almost undetectable events. As would be expected, the more obvious the prompt, the more dependent the student is on the instructor. Conversely, the less obvious the prompt, the more the student must take responsibility to initiate the behavior.

Whenever you use prompts, you should begin with those prompts that will ensure that the desired behavior will occur. These beginning prompts are likely to be very obvious to the student and involve your active participation. In general, it is a good idea to use all three types of prompts when you begin teaching a new skill. Then over time you will fade them.

FADING

Fading is the gradual removal of a prompt.

Fading is used to foster independence by reducing or eliminating the control that the prompter (instructor) and prompts have had over the student's behavior. Thus, fading is really the elimination of the control of the prompt (or the gradual change of the prompt). It should be noted that not all of the discriminative stimuli are faded, only those prompts delivered by the instructor. Consider the student discussed earlier who had his pants around his knees. Our task as instructors is merely to fade all verbal, gestural, and physical prompts associated with having him raise his pants so that the naturally occurring stimuli associated with pants raising will cue him to do so. In other words, we want the student to be cued to raise his pants by the pants around his ankles and by being in the bedroom. Ideally we want his pants around his ankles to be the ultimate, long-lasting, naturally occurring cue for pants raising.

Fading is accomplished by providing the student with a less obvious or active prompt than you had given him previously. For example, the first time you prompt a student to raise his pants, you may have to guide his hands to the waistband and then guide him in raising his pants. The next time you prompt him, you may only guide his hands to the waistband. Thus, you will have gone from actually physically guiding the student in raising his pants to just placing his hands on the waistband. Eventually, of course, you will fade all prompts so that the student raises his pants himself.

How to Fade Prompts

There are two ways to fade a verbal prompt. First, you can simply reduce the number of words in the instruction, e.g., from "James, pants up," to "pants up." Although this simple instruction somewhat resembles an animal training command, keep in mind that it's being used to produce independence of action by the student and to avoid confusing him and thereby retarding his educational progress. Second, you can speak more softly each time so that the student must pay more attention to what you are saying. It's possible to fade a verbal prompt in this fashion to a point where the student must practically read your lips.

Gestural prompts are faded in two ways. First, the size of the gesture can be reduced, e.g., from a sweeping motion of your arm and pointing to just pointing. Second, a less obvious gesture can be used, e.g., looking rather than pointing.

Physical prompts are the most difficult to fade because they involve actually touching the student, who can easily tell whether or not you are touching him. Thus, the transition from touching to not touching is difficult to make. Fortunately, there are four ways to overcome this problem. The first is to progressively reduce the amount of the touch, say, from touching the student with your hand, to touching the student with only a part of your hand, to touching the student with just your fingers, to just touching the student with one finger. The second way is to progressively reduce the amount of pressure associated with the touch so that less pressure is used on each succeeding prompting trial. The third way is to move the location of where you touch the student away from the focal point of the behavior, perhaps progressively moving your touch further up the student's arm away from his hands when you are prompting pants raising. You would still be physically prompting pants raising, but the student would be required to use his hands without their being touched. The fourth and final way is to use all three types of prompts in the beginning of training and fade the physical prompts first while retaining the gestural and verbal prompts. Gestural and verbal prompts are faded last because they are easier to fade.

Practice Set 7A

Answer the following questions.

1. Why is a prompt considered to be an auxiliary discriminative stimulus?
2. Below is a list of common prompts. Label each one according to whether it is a physical, gestural, or verbal prompt.
    a. "Do this."
    b. Guiding a student's hand to pick up a ball
    c. Pointing to the door
    d. Holding up a picture of a cat
    e. "Stand by Dennis."
    f. Looking downward at the student's pants
    g. Touching a student's shoulder
3. What technique is used to prevent the student from becoming dependent on a prompt?
4. What kind of prompt should you use to begin training a student?
5. What are two ways of fading a verbal prompt?
6. What are two ways of fading a gestural prompt?
7. What are four ways of dealing with the problem of fading physical prompts?
8. Ms. Essex said, "Hand me the sock," and guided Marvin's hand to the sock. Did Ms. Essex use prompts?

Answers are found on pages 199 and 200.

PROMPTING AND FADING

Now let's see how prompting and fading can be used together to form effective programs for teaching students to perform behaviors independently.

Examples of Prompting and Fading

The first example of prompting and fading comes from a toilet training program for retarded persons.* The first part of the table lists the general guidelines to follow in using prompts to shape a student to use the toilet. The second part presents the toileting prompts and the order in which they are faded. Note that all three types of prompts are used in the beginning, that the prompts become less obvious over the successive training sessions, and that the physical prompts are faded first.

TOILET-APPROACH PROMPTS

GENERAL GUIDELINES

1. Determine the minimal prompt the student responds to. This may be a touch, pointing toward the toilet, or an instruction.
2. Use a less active prompt the next time the student is prompted to the toilet.
3. Wait a few seconds after the prompt before giving it again.
4. The sequence of toileting prompts is listed below from most active to least active. The student will usually begin independently toileting himself before the least active prompt is given.

SEQUENCE OF STEPS

	Prompt	Example
1.	Verbal prompt +	"John, go to the toilet."
	Gestural prompt +	Point to the toilet.
	Physical prompt	Lightly tug at the student's shirt (guide him from his chair to the toilet if necessary).
2.	Verbal prompt +	"John, go to the toilet."
	Gestural prompt No physical prompt	Point to the toilet.

---

*Adapted with permission from *Toilet Training the retarded: A rapid program for day and nighttime independent toileting* by R. M. Foxx and N. H. Azrin. Champaign, Ill.: Research Press, 1973, pp. 42-43.

3. Reduced verbal prompt   "John, toilet."
    +
    Gestural prompt   Point to the toilet.
    No physical prompt

4. Reduced verbal prompt   "Toilet."
    +
    Gestural prompt   Point to the toilet.
    No physical prompt

5. No verbal prompt
    Gestural prompt   Point to the toilet with your arm
    No physical prompt   fully extended and motion toward
                                   the toilet with your head.

6. No verbal prompt
    Reduced gestural prompt   Point to the toilet with your arm
    No physical prompt   partially extended and full head
                                   motion.

7. No verbal prompt
    Reduced gestural prompt   Fully swing your head toward the
    (no arm motion)   toilet.
    No physical prompt

8. No verbal prompt
    Reduced gestural prompt   Slightly motion toward the toilet
    No physical prompt   with your head.

9. No verbal prompt
    Reduced gestural prompt   Move your eyes toward the toilet.
    (no head motion)
    No physical prompt

Regarding whether or not the student will ever toilet himself without a prompt, Foxx and Azrin state:

> When the trainer has reached the phase where slight arm, head, and eye movements are effective, the fading process will usually occur naturally thereafter without the need for the trainer to consciously decrease the size of the gesture. This natural fading occurs because the trainer's head and arms are normally moving about. Consequently, the gestural prompt blends naturally into this movement background and the resident is less able to depend on the movements as a reminder of the trainer's desires. He then begins relying on his own memory and desires. (pp. 40-41)

Now let's look at the shaping program for teaching students to raise and lower their pants that was developed for the toilet training program.*

PROMPTS FOR RAISING AND LOWERING PANTS

GENERAL GUIDELINES

1. Determine the minimal prompt the student responds to. This may be a touch, pointing to his pants, or a verbal instruction.
2. Use a less active prompt the next time the student is prompted to pull his pants up or down.
3. Wait a few seconds after the prompt before giving it again.
4. The sequence of dressing prompts is listed below from most active to least active. The student will usually begin independently raising or lowering his pants before the least active prompt is given.

SEQUENCE OF STEPS FOR PULLING PANTS DOWN

Note: The student should pull his pants down below his knees.

	Prompt	Example
1.	Verbal prompt	"John, pants down."
	+	
	Gestural prompt	Point to the student's pants.
	+	
	Physical prompt	Grasp the student's hands around the waistband of his pants and guide him in pulling them down.
2.	Reduced verbal prompt	"Pants down."
	+	
	Gestural prompt	Point to the student's pants.
	+	
	Physical prompt	Grasp the student's hands around the waistband of his pants if necessary and guide him in pulling them down.
3.	Reduced verbal prompt	"Down."
	+	
	Gestural prompt	Point to the student's pants.
	+	
	Reduced physical prompt	Guide the student's hands to the waistband of his pants if necessary.

---

*Adapted with permission from *Toilet Training the retarded: A rapid program for day and nighttime independent toileting* by R. M. Foxx and N. H. Azrin. Champaign, Ill.: Research Press, 1973, pp. 42-43.

4. Verbal prompt   "Down."
    +
    Reduced gestural prompt   Look at the student's pants.
    +
    Physical prompt,   Guide the student's hands to the
    if necessary   waistband of his pants if necessary.

5. No verbal prompt
    Reduced gestural prompt   Look at the student's pants.
    No physical prompt

SEQUENCE OF STEPS FOR PULLING PANTS UP

Note: Since the student's pants are below his knees, it will be easier for him
to pull them up if he bends forward slightly.

	Prompt	Example
1.	Verbal prompt + Gestural prompt + Physical prompt	"John, pants up." Point to the student's pants. Place your hands over the student's hands and guide his hands to grasp the waistband of his pants and to pull them up.
2.	Reduced verbal prompt + Gestural prompt + Physical prompt	"Pants up." Point to the student's pants. Grasp the student's hands around the waistband of his pants and guide him in pulling them up.
3.	Reduced verbal prompt + Gestural prompt + Reduced physical prompt	"Up." Point to the student's pants. Guide the student's hands to the waistband if necessary.
4.	Verbal prompt + Reduced gestural prompt + Physical prompt, if necessary	"Up." Look at the student's pants. Guide the student's hands to the waistband if necessary.
5.	No verbal prompt Gestural prompt No physical prompt	Look at the student's pants.

Again, note that the prompting steps were sequenced so that the most obvious prompts occurred first, followed by less obvious prompts each time (the prompts were faded). In many cases, the student will begin raising and lowering his pants himself before you reach Step 5.

In Chapter 6, we described a procedure to shape Merle's eye contact. Prompting was used in this program whenever the instructor said, "Merle, look at me" and held the peanut to her eyes. Obviously, it is cumbersome, unrealistic, and unnatural for the instructor to keep lifting the peanut to her eyes each time she wants Merle to look at her. To solve this problem, the instructor will fade holding the peanut near her eyes because it, in large part, is controlling Merle's eye contact, more so than the verbal prompt.

To fade holding the peanut near her eyes, the instructor uses the following fading procedure. After Merle reliably gives her 2 seconds of eye contact (the terminal response), she raises the peanut to her eyes but cups it in her hand so that it's not visible. Over successive eye contact trials, the instructor lifts the peanut (hidden behind her fingers) to slightly below her eyes, to her cheek, to her chin, to her throat, to her chest, to her side, and ultimately to where she can say, "Merle, look at me" and take the peanut from the bowl and place it in his mouth. Thus, she ends the fading program at an ideal spot. Now whenever she requests eye contact, she can simply wait for Merle to look at her and then give him a peanut from either a bowl or a pocket in her apron. At this point, she can begin the generalization training of eye contact outside the training area (see Chapters 6 and 13).

Cardinal Rules for Prompting and Fading

Prompting and fading require a great deal of expertise on your part and the only way to gain this expertise is by using the techniques as often as possible. To use prompting and fading correctly, you must prompt the student regularly during the initial training phases and not at all during the final phases. Otherwise, the student becomes dependent on you and the prompts. (This is one of the major problems of retarded students: they are highly dependent on prompts. Even when you know they know what to do, they still wait to be prompted.) Thus, it is important that you make steady progress in fading the prompts.

There are three cardinal rules to follow when you use prompting and fading.

1. *Do not use a prompt that has been faded.* In other words, once a student has correctly responded to a less obvious prompt,

don't return to an earlier level of prompt (more obvious prompt) that has been faded. To do so would retard the training because the student would become more dependent on you and the more obvious prompt.

2. *Always begin each training session or day by using the prompts that the student successfully responded to at the end of the previous session or day.* This will start the new session or day with a successful effort and will take care of any possible memory lapses the student may have had.

3. *Always remain within arm's reach of the student during the initial stages of training.* This is done so that you can provide a physical prompt or guidance whenever needed.

Practice Set 7B

Answer the following questions.

1. Arrange the following prompts into a sequence of steps that would permit fading to be accomplished easily.
    a. "Zack, take a bite," point to the bowl of food
    b. "Zack, bite," point to the bowl of food
    c. "Zack, take a bite," point to the bowl of food, touch Zack's hand that holds the spoon
    d. "Zack, take a bite," point to the bowl of food, guide Zack's hand to the spoon
    e. "Zack, take bite," point to the bowl of food
    f. Point to the bowl of food
    g. "Zack," point to the bowl of food

2. During speech training sessions with George, Ms. Tuttle had been holding an edible near her mouth so that George would look at her mouth as she formed the words. Now that George reliably looks at her mouth, how should Ms. Tuttle fade holding the edible near her mouth?

3. At the end of yesterday's shaping session to teach Sidney to walk, Mr. Pares had gotten Sidney to respond to the verbal prompt "Walk" paired with a "come here" motion in which Mr. Pares pointed to the spot where he wanted Sidney to walk. Mr. Pares would like to begin the day by eliminating the gestural prompt. Should he?

4. During today's session, Sidney has responded to the verbal prompt "Walk" on two occasions. Mr. Pares has just given that prompt again, but Sidney has not moved. Mr. Pares is growing anxious and thinks that maybe he should resume using the gestural prompt that had worked before. What do you think of Mr. Pares' idea?

5. Today Ms. Saunders will teach Ann to brush her hair. She is standing 6 feet away from Ann when she gives her the verbal prompt to brush her hair. Ann looks at her but does not respond. What cardinal rule of prompting has Ms. Saunders violated?

The answers are on page 200.

SUMMARY

The use of auxiliary discriminative stimuli to cue a student to perform a particular behavior is called prompting, and the discriminative stimuli themselves are called prompts. The importance of prompts is that they greatly increase the likelihood that the desired behavior will occur. There are three types of prompts: verbal, gestural, and physical. High functioning students may only need prompting for the first few training trials; lower functioning students may need it for many. Training always should begin with prompts that will ensure that the desired behavior will occur, and these prompts will often be obvious ones.

Fading is the gradual removal of a prompt. It fosters independence by shifting the responsibility for performing a behavior from the prompt and prompter (instructor) to the student. Fading is accomplished by providing the student with a less obvious or active prompt than she had been given previously. Verbal prompts can be faded by reducing the number of words used or speaking progressively more softly, while gestural prompts can be faded by reducing the size of the gesture or using a less obvious gesture. Physical prompts are difficult to fade, but they can be faded in four ways: by progressively reducing the size of the area touched; by slowly lessening the pressure used; by gradually moving the location of the touch away from the focal point of the behavior; and by initially training with all three types of prompts and then fading the physical one while retaining the gestural and verbal ones.

To use prompting and fading correctly within a behavior shaping program, three cardinal rules must be followed: (1) once a prompt has been faded, it must not be given again, (2) each training session or day must begin with the prompts to which the student responded successfully at the end of the previous session or day, and (3) the instructor must remain within arm's reach of the student during the initial stages of training, in case a physical prompt or guidance is needed.

SUGGESTED READINGS

Foxx, R. M., & Azrin, N. H. *Toilet training the retarded: A rapid program for day and nighttime independent toileting.* Champaign, Ill.: Research Press, 1973.

Rincover, A. Variables affecting stimulus fading and discriminative responding in psychotic children. *Journal of Abnormal Psychology*, 1978, *87*, 541-553.

Schreibman, L. Effects of within-stimulus and extra-stimulus-prompting or discrimination learning in autistic children. *Journal of Applied Behavior Analysis*, 1975, *8*, 91-112.

Sidman, M., & Stoddard, L. T. The effectiveness of fading in programming a simultaneous form of discrimination for retarded children. *Journal of the Experimental Analysis of Behavior*, 1967, *10*, 3-15.

Walsh, B. F., & Lamberts, F. Errorless discrimination and picture fading as techniques for teaching sight words to TMR students. *American Journal of Mental Deficiency*, 1979, *83*, 473-479.

Review Set 7

1. A p_____ is an auxiliary discriminative stimulus.
2. The three types of prompts are p_____, v_____, and g_____.
3. F_____ is the gradual removal of a prompt.
4. The p_____ prompt is the most difficult prompt to fade.
5. Fading is used to foster independence by eliminating the control that the p_____ and p_____ have had over the student's behavior.
6. Fading is accomplished by providing the student with a less o_____ or a_____ prompt than you had given him previously.

Answers are found on page 200.

CHAPTER 8

Modeling and Imitation

Severely and profoundly retarded individuals have limited receptive language which, of course, is why we use prompts to facilitate their acquisition of new behaviors. As discussed in the previous chapter, verbal instructions or prompts alone usually aren't sufficient to cue the severely handicapped person to perform the desired behavior. In such cases, we combine gestural and physical prompts with the verbal prompt in order to maximize the chances that the student will perform the requested behavior. We'll now consider *imitative prompts*, which are a special type of prompt that is especially useful for teaching individuals who fail to respond adequately to verbal instructions. They require that the student learn to imitate and eventually generalize this imitation to new behaviors, which in turn facilitates the learning of new skills. A three-part procedure is given for training imitative behavior, and the use of reinforcement and prompting to bring about generalized imitation is explained. Three ways to maximize the success of training procedures also are listed.

IMITATION

There are two behavioral principles underlying the use of imitative prompts: *modeling* and *imitation*.

> Imitation is the response of matching the behavior of a model.

Imitation is basic to most learning, since most of what we learn comes from watching others. These others, in effect, serve as models for the imitated behavior. We begin imitating as in-

95

fants and never stop. For example, an infant learns to smile and coo from watching her parents smile and coo at her. Her parents are modeling for her since they want her to imitate them. Or, as the child grows older, she may join her mother in a game of pat-a-cake or peek-a-boo. The infant or child imitates because imitation is reinforced. A child who imitates a parent is heavily reinforced with attention, hugs, and a continuation of the action or game that is being imitated. Eventually the child will engage in *generalized imitation*, which means that she will imitate a behavior without ever having received reinforcement for imitating it. A child who engages in generalized imitation is well on her way to learning much about her world.

Imitation continues into adulthood but the manner in which it's practiced changes. As adults we often imitate the behavior or appearance of high status figures or celebrities. This explains why many women wear their hair like certain movie stars, or why a number of men wear football jerseys displaying the numbers of famous pro players.

In addition to all of their behavioral and intellectual deficits, severely and profoundly retarded students do not imitate very well. This deficit not only prevents them from learning new skills but also from being very reinforcing. (Many parents of severely handicapped children will confirm that a child who does not imitate daddy or mommy is not very reinforcing to be with.)

IMITATIVE PROMPTS

> An imitative prompt is a discriminative stimulus
> provided by a model in which the model's behavior
> is to be imitated.

It's crucial that your students learn to imitate. To teach them, use an imitation training procedure consisting of three parts:

1. Provide a model or a combination of a model and prompting of the behavior you wish the student to imitate.
2. Observe the student to determine whether the student has imitated the model's behavior.
3. Reinforce the imitated behavior.

The standard method of conducting imitation training is to present a verbal prompt or instruction to the student, such as "Touch your nose," together with a demonstration of the behavior, such as touching your nose as you give the instruction.

If the behavior is already in the student's behavioral repertoire, then she is likely to do it and you can provide reinforcement. If the behavior is not in the student's repertoire, then you'll probably have to shape it and use generous amounts of gestural and physical prompts.

Let's look at an example of imitation training. Ms. Rogers would like to begin to teach Art his body parts. She decides to begin by teaching him to touch his head. She'll use an imitation training procedure and his favorite candy, jelly beans, to reinforce his imitation. Ms. Rogers begins by saying, "Art, do this" (a verbal prompt) and touching the top of her head (modeling the behavior). Because Art has never before received imitation training, he doesn't respond to Ms. Rogers' modeling of the behavior. As a result, Ms. Rogers decides to physically guide (physically prompt) Art in touching the top of his head. So she says, "Do this," touches the top of her head with her right hand, and uses her left hand to guide Art's right hand in touching the top of his head. As soon as his hand reaches his head, she takes a jelly bean out of her apron pocket and reinforces Art, saying, "Good, Art. Good touching your head." Eventually she fades out the physical guidance so that Art is responding solely to her instructions and modeling of the behavior. When he will reliably imitate her by touching his head when she touches hers, she will switch to modeling touching her nose.

Ms. Rogers' imitation training procedure consisted of

1. Gaining Art's attention by speaking his name
2. Giving him the verbal prompt "Do this"
3. Modeling the behavior, that is, touching her head
4. Providing a physical prompt during the initial stages of training, that is, guiding his hand in touching his head
5. Reinforcing the imitative behavior

Practice Set 8A

Design a brief imitation training program for each of the following students. (Assume that no physical guidance will be necessary.)

1. Cindy is to touch her ear.

    What will the instructor (model) do?

    What will the instructor say?

    What will Cindy be expected to do?

    What will happen if Cindy performs correctly?

2. Sandy will clap her hands.
   What will the instructor do?
   What will the instructor say?
   What will Sandy be expected to do?
   What will happen if Sandy performs correctly?

The answers are on pages 200 and 201.

GENERALIZED IMITATION

It is important that the imitative behavior always be reinforced. By doing so, you will not only be strengthening that specific imitated behavior but will be increasing the likelihood that generalized imitation will occur. You may remember that generalized imitation occurs when a person performs an imitated response or behavior that has never been reinforced. For instance, Ms. Rogers has systematically taught Art to touch his head, nose, ears, eyes, and mouth through her imitation training program and liberal use of jelly beans. Now she'll ask Art to imitate a behavior she has never modeled before. She takes her right hand and touches her left arm, and says, "Art, do this." To her delight, Art touches his arm. Art has just performed a generalized imitative behavior. Naturally she reinforces this performance.

What has happened is that Art has received reinforcement for imitating in the past and has generalized in that he expects to be reinforced each time he is asked to imitate. Thus, the use of reinforcement when teaching one imitative behavior increases the likelihood that other imitative behaviors will increase as well.

You may be wondering whether it is better to give the general instruction "Do this" or the more specific instruction that describes the exact behavior to be performed, such as "Touch your mouth." In general, use of the general instruction "Do this" is more likely to produce generalized imitation. However, for very low functioning students it's usually best to provide an instruction that describes the exact behavior you wish to be imitated in order to avoid confusing the student. The best advice is to start off the instruction with "Do this" (and physical guidance or prompting if necessary). If the student imitates your modeled behavior, then continue to use that instruction. If, on the other hand, after several training trials the student fails to imitate (even with physical guidance provided), then switch to using a verbal instruction that describes the specific behavior you want the student to imitate.

Imitation training plays a major role in shaping speech in severely and profoundly handicapped students. The program described next illustrates the use of imitation training within a speech shaping program. (Fading will be illustrated as well.)

AN EXAMPLE OF IMITATION TRAINING

Remember Merle, the student whose eye contact was shaped in the previous chapter? We'll now see how Merle can be shaped to make an "Mm" sound.

Behind a partition in the corner of the classroom, the instructor and Merle are seated at a table facing each other. A bowl of peanuts is located to the instructor's right and out of Merle's reach. In front of the instructor is a recording sheet and a pencil. The instructor begins by taking a peanut out of the bowl and placing it in Merle's mouth. She does this several times until Merle's eyes track the peanut from the bowl to his mouth. The instructor is now ready to shape the "Mm" sound because Merle is intently tracking the peanut in her hand with his eyes. The next time she reaches for a peanut, she lifts the peanut to her mouth. As Merle's eyes follow the peanut to her mouth, she says, "Merle, say 'Mm' " and she forms her lips and says "Mm." As soon as his mouth forms the "Mm" sound, she quickly places the peanut in his mouth, strokes his cheek, and says, "Good saying 'Mm,' Merle." She then scores a correct response on her recording sheet.

Each speech shaping session consists of 20 trials and there are 100 trials each day. The use of five sessions throughout the day eliminates the possibility that Merle will become bored or satiated (see Chapter 3). Once Merle has imitated his instructor by forming his lips to approximate the "Mm" sound 90% of the time or better over 20 trials, the instructor is ready to require Merle to make a sound when his lips are pursed. Now when she says, "Merle, say 'Mm,' " he must make a sound. If Merle makes a sound, she reinforces him as before.

Once Merle has made a sound, the instructor gradually changes the criterion for reinforcement (shapes) until Merle imitates her by saying "Mm." When Merle doesn't respond within 5 seconds of the verbal prompt and imitative prompt, she returns the peanut to the bowl and records an incorrect response on her recording sheet. The speech shaping program ends when Merle will say "Mm" on at least 45 of 50 trials (90% or better). At that point, the instructor is ready to begin reinforcing Merle's "Mm" sound intermittently so that it will be maintained in his behavioral repertoire. After that she'll begin shaping a new sound such as "Ba" while occasionally requiring him to say "Mm." Much later, she'll fade holding the peanut near her mouth, because it is controlling Merle's speech as much as the verbal and imitative prompts.

To fade holding the peanut near her mouth, the instructor uses the following fading procedure. She raises the peanut to her mouth but cups it in her hand so that it's not visible. Over successive speech trials, she lifts the peanut (hidden behind her fingers) to slightly below her eyes, to her cheek, to her chin, to her throat, to her chest, to her side, and ultimately to where she can say, "Merle, say ___" and take the peanut from the bowl and place it in his mouth. Thus, she ends the fading program at an ideal spot. Now whenever she requests Merle to imitate a speech sound, she can simply wait for Merle to say the sound and then give him a peanut from either a bowl or a pocket in her apron. The same overall program would be used if Merle functioned at a high enough level to be shaped to say words such as "mama" rather than simply sounds.

Practice Set 8B

For each statement, identify the modeled behavior, the imitated behavior, the imitative prompt, any other prompts that were used, and the reinforcer(s).

1. Mr. Stone lifted his arm, said, "Michele, do this," and gave Michele a gumdrop when she imitated.
2. Ms. Rendleman tapped the table, said, "Leon, tap the table," guided Leon's hand to the table, and gave him a hug and a bit of pecan.
3. Ms. Edmonds rolled the ball, said, "Bev, do this," and touched a vibrator to Bev's arm after she had imitated.
4. Dr. Henson formed the "K" sound with his lips, said, "Don, say 'Ka,'" and gave Don a sip of decaffeinated coffee when he said "Ka."

Answers are found on page 201.

WAYS TO MAXIMIZE SUCCESSFUL IMITATION TRAINING

You can maximize the success of your imitation training programs by following these guidelines.

1. Always begin a training session by having the student perform a previously imitated behavior first.

2. Once the student has successfully imitated a few behaviors, alternate your presentation of imitative prompts to keep the student's interest.
3. Have people serve as models that the student likes.

SUMMARY

Imitation is the response of matching the behavior of a model, and it is an essential skill for many types of learning. An imitative prompt is a discriminative stimulus provided by a model in which the model's behavior serves as the behavior to be imitated. Imitative prompts are used to show the student the behavior you would like him to imitate. Imitation is taught through imitation training, which consists of three parts: (1) providing a model or a combination of a model and prompting of the behavior the student is to imitate, (2) observing whether the student has imitated the model's behavior, and (3) reinforcing the imitated behavior. Generalized imitation occurs when a student imitates a modeled behavior that he has never before been reinforced for imitating. Providing reinforcement during imitation training and using a general verbal prompt increase the likelihood that generalized imitation will occur.

When conducting imitation training, you must (1) gain the student's attention, (2) give a verbal instruction such as "Do this," (3) perform the action you want the student to imitate, (4) use a physical prompt during the initial stages if necessary, and (5) reinforce the imitated behavior. The success of your training can be maximized by following three guidelines: (1) begin the training session with a previously imitated behavior, (2) alternate the presentation of imitative prompts after the student has successfully imitated a few behaviors, and (3) have people that the student likes model the behaviors to be imitated.

SUGGESTED READINGS

Baer, D. M., & Sherman, J. A. Reinforcement control of generalized imitation in young children. *Journal of Experimental Child Psychology*, 1964, *1*, 37-49.

Lovaas, O. I., Freitag, K., Nelson, K., & Whalen, C. The establishment of imitation and its use for the development of complex behavior in schizophrenic children. *Behaviour Research and Therapy*, 1967, *5*, 171-182.

Metz, J. R. Conditioning generalized imitation in autistic children. *Journal of Experimental Child Psychology*, 1965, *2*, 389-399.

Steinman, W. M. The social control of generalized imitation. *Journal of Applied Behavior Analysis*, 1970, *3*, 159-167.

Review Set 8

1. An i_____ prompt is a way of showing a student what you would like her to do.

2. I_____ is the response of matching the behavior of a model.

3. When a person imitates a behavior that she has never before been reinforced for imitating, we say that g_____ imitation has occurred.

4. An i_____ prompt is a discriminative stimulus provided by a model.

5. The individual who provides the imitative prompt is called the m_____.

6. R_____ should be provided during imitation training in order to increase the likelihood that generalized imitation will occur.

7. Three ways to maximize the success of your imitation training program are to begin each session with a p_____ imitated behavior, a_____ prompts after the student has imitated a few behaviors, and have people that the student l_____ model behaviors.

Answers are found on page 201.

CHAPTER 9

The Task Analysis Model
and Stimulus-Response Chains

In the preceding chapters you've learned various teaching techniques: shaping, prompting and fading, and modeling and imitation. However, to teach your students well, you also need to know how to structure your teaching programs for individual students. This means knowing how to determine two things: (1) the sequence of steps (behaviors) that lead to the achievement of the behavioral objective, and (2) the current ability level (entry behavior) of the student. These determinations can be made by using the *task analysis* model.

> A task analysis is a detailed description of each behavior needed to accomplish a behavioral objective given the student's current ability level.

We'll show you two methods of determining the exact sequence of steps for achieving an objective and discuss even finer divisions of steps into behavior chains. The roles of conditioned reinforcers and discriminative stimuli in behavior chains will be explained, and the uses of forward and backward chaining will be described. Finally, we'll tell you how to determine where your student should begin on any given sequence of steps.

SEQUENCE OF STEPS

A task analysis has three main components: a description of the behavioral objective or goal; a detailed description of each behavior or step needed to accomplish the objective; and an assessment of the student's entry behavior or current ability level. You've already learned how to determine the behavioral objective (see Chapter 1). We're now going to consider the second task analysis component: determining the sequence of steps (behaviors) needed to accomplish the objective.

Task Analyses of Behavior Sequences

A task analysis contains the sequence or chain of behaviors needed to accomplish an objective. (Stimulus-response or behavior chains will be described later in this chapter.) Each step in the sequence must specify, *in order*, the exact behavior the student must perform to attain the stated behavioral objective.

To understand task analysis better, let's take a task that you perform. Any one of the myriad tasks that you perform each day can be broken down into steps. For example, an important daily task is brushing your teeth. When you first learned to brush your teeth, your parents described and/or demonstrated a sequence of steps for you to follow. Let's look at a sample task analysis showing the steps for toothbrushing.

Task Analysis of Brushing Teeth

Step 1	Pick up toothpaste tube
Step 2	Unscrew toothpaste tube cap and set it aside
Step 3	Pick up toothbrush
Step 4	Squeeze toothpaste onto toothbrush bristles
Step 5	Set toothbrush down
Step 6	Replace toothpaste tube cap and set tube down
Step 7	Pick up toothbrush and place toothbrush bristles on teeth
Step 8	Make scrubbing, brushing motions in order to cleanse all teeth
Step 9	Remove toothbrush from mouth
Step 10	Turn on cold water
Step 11	Spit toothpaste into sink
Step 12	Pick up cup and fill with water
Step 13	Fill mouth with water from cup and set cup aside
Step 14	Swish water in mouth, then spit water into sink
Step 15	Rinse toothbrush under running water
Step 16	Turn off water and place toothbrush in holder
Step 17	Dry face and hands with towel
Step 18	Put away toothpaste

Almost everyone with normal intelligence learns a toothbrushing routine with little difficulty after the behavior chain involved has been described or demonstrated to him. The learner either remembers what he was told or shown or logically determines the behavioral sequence. Retarded students, however, often don't have good memories and usually can't figure out the next step. In fact, the instructor may have to spend many trials teaching the student just one of the steps. For such students, accurate sequencing of the educational tasks is crucial. Because a task analysis outlines each step in its proper sequence, it provides the instructor with a guide for helping students to accomplish an objective.

To determine the sequence of steps in a task you can rely on your memory and list the sequence of behaviors or physically perform each behavior and list that behavior immediately after you perform it. Obviously, writing a sequence of steps from memory offers the advantage of requiring little time and no special environment or equipment. For instance, a task analysis of toothbrushing is easier and faster to do from memory than going to the bathroom and listing each behavior while you brush your teeth. But a possible problem in listing a sequence of steps in a task from memory is that some steps or details may be overlooked. For example, when writing the sequence of behaviors that comprise toothbrushing, it's easy for a normal person to forget a small detail such as that the toothbrush is to be held with the bristles facing upward when the toothpaste is squeezed from the tube. Yet this can be a difficult discrimination for some retarded students. The advantage of physically performing each behavior in the sequence is that you'll be more likely to include all the necessary steps and details that apply to your students. You can simply stop after each step and decide which aspects of the step are crucial for any given student.

To decide which method to try in listing any particular sequence of steps in a task, ask yourself the following questions:

1. Are you familiar with the objective, that is, do you perform the task regularly?
2. Is there a likelihood that you might omit a step or crucial detail?
3. Is any special equipment or area needed?

If you answered yes to the first question and answered no to the others, then using your memory would probably suffice. Otherwise you should physically perform the steps in the task.

Practice Set 9A

Answer the following questions.

1. A t_____ a_____ is a detailed description of each behavior needed to accomplish an objective given the student's current ability level.

2. Each step in a sequence of behaviors must specify, in o_____, the exact behavior the student must perform.

3. The sequence of steps needed to accomplish the behavioral objective can be determined in what two ways?

4. What is the disadvantage in relying on your memory to sequence the steps in a task?

5. What are the three questions you should ask yourself to decide which method to try in listing the steps in a task?

Answers are found on pages 201 and 202.

Behavior Chains (Stimulus-Response Chains)

> A behavior (stimulus-response) chain is a sequence of stimuli and responses that ends with a terminal reinforcer.

Most of our behavior doesn't consist of simple responses followed by reinforcers, as described by the three-term contingency or instructional cycle. Rather, we engage in a series or sequence of responses (a behavior chain) that results in some important reinforcer at the end of the sequence. Because the reinforcer comes at the end of the sequence, it's called a *terminal reinforcer* (SR^+). Examples of behavior chains that you perform include shopping, bathing, going out for the evening, driving to work, and bowling.

We perform these long sequences (chains) of behavior even though the reinforcer only appears at the end of the behavior chain. We do so because of conditioned reinforcement. Each response in the chain is followed by an event (a stimulus) that reinforces that response (conditioned reinforcement) while simultaneously serving as a discriminative stimulus for the next response. A discriminative stimulus is also a *conditioned reinforcer* (Sr^+) because it is a previously neutral stimulus that has acquired its reinforcing properties from being repeatedly paired with a reinforcer. Thus, a stimulus in a behavior chain serves a dual role. It's a conditioned reinforcer (S^{r+}) for the response (R) it follows and a discriminative stimulus (S^D) for the response it precedes. In its role as a conditioned reinforcer, the stimulus maintains and strengthens the response it follows; in its role as a discriminative stimulus, it ensures that the next response in the chain will occur. Let's look at a common behavior—eating at a fast food restaurant—as a stimulus-response (S-R) chain.

(1) $S^D \rightarrow$ (2) $R \rightarrow$ (3) $S^D \rightarrow$ (4) $R \rightarrow$
(restaurant   (drive into   (door of   (enter
sign)   parking lot)   restaurant)   restaurant)

(5) $S^D \rightarrow$ (6) $R \rightarrow$ (7) $S^D \rightarrow$ (8) $R \rightarrow$
(counter)   (walk to   (menu on   (read menu)
counter)   wall)

(9) $S^D \rightarrow$ (10) $R \rightarrow$ (11) $S^D \rightarrow$ (12) $R \rightarrow$
(counter   (order food)   (food on tray)   (pay counter
employee)   ("That will be   employee)
("May I take $1.98, please.")
your order?")

(13) $S^D \rightarrow$ (14) $R \rightarrow$ (15) $S^D \rightarrow$ (16) $R \rightarrow$
(food on tray)   (carry food   (food on table)   (eat)
to table)

S^{R+}
(delicious food)

As the example shows, the promise of delicious food at the end of the chain is sufficient to produce a number of responses and these responses are reinforced by the discriminative stimuli that follow each of them along the way.

We can now see that a task analysis is nothing more than a specification of the responses in a behavior chain that must be performed in order to reach the behavioral objective. The behavioral objective is typically the last response in the behavior chain. The reinforcer that's delivered when the objective is accomplished is simply the terminal reinforcer (S^{R+}) at the end of the behavior chain.

Let's take the behavioral objective of teaching a student to shampoo her hair and express this objective as a behavior chain. A task analysis reveals that the following behaviors are necessary in order to accomplish the objective:

1. Wet hair
2. Apply shampoo to hair

3. Work shampoo into a lather
4. Rinse hair
5. Dry hair

Now look at the task analysis as a behavior or stimulus-response (S-R) chain.

(1) $S^D \rightarrow$ (sink)

(2) $R \rightarrow$ (walk to sink)

(3) $S^D \rightarrow$ (faucet)

(4) $R \rightarrow$ (turn on faucet)

(5) $S^D \rightarrow$ (water running)

(6) $R \rightarrow$ (wet hair under faucet)

(7) $S^D \rightarrow$ (wet hair)

(8) $R \rightarrow$ (pick up shampoo bottle)

(9) $S^D \rightarrow$ (shampoo bottle in hand)

(10) $R \rightarrow$ (open cap of shampoo)

(11) $S^D \rightarrow$ (open bottle of shampoo)

(12) $R \rightarrow$ (apply shampoo to hair)

(13) $S^D \rightarrow$ (shampoo in hair)

(14) $R \rightarrow$ (work shampoo into lather)

(15) $S^D \rightarrow$ (lather in hair)

(16) $R \rightarrow$ (rinse hair)

(17) $S^D \rightarrow$ (wet hair)

(18) $R \rightarrow$ (pick up towel)

(19) $S^D \rightarrow$ (towel in hand)

(20) $R \rightarrow$ (dry hair)

(21) $S^D \rightarrow$ (wet towel)

(22) $R \rightarrow$ (hang up towel)

(23) $S^D \rightarrow$ (open bottle of shampoo)

(24) $R \rightarrow$ (replace cap on shampoo bottle)

S^{R+}

(praise from instructor, an edible, and a hug or pat)

In this example, we can see the difference between a task analysis and a behavior or stimulus-response chain. The task analysis merely specified 5 responses (tasks) that had to be performed in order to accomplish the behavioral objective of shampooing, whereas the behavior chain specified 12 responses. Furthermore, the task analysis didn't specify the discriminative stimuli that preceded or followed each response, whereas the behavior chain did. There is an explanation for this difference.

The task analysis of shampooing was based on the fact that the student had all of the necessary responses in her behavioral repertoire. Thus, the behavioral objective, shampooing, could be accomplished by simply chaining or sequencing the responses so that each followed the other until the objective was achieved. However, if she hadn't had the necessary responses in her behavioral repertoire, as is almost always the case for severely and profoundly retarded students, the task analysis would have been of little use. (This is why great care should be exercised in selecting books that claim to contain task analyses or curricula for severely handicapped students. Many are of little value because they only list a number of global responses or steps rather than breaking each task down into a behavior chain that shows *all* the stimuli and responses necessary to achieve the behavioral objective.) Thus, you should consider a task analysis as simply the first step in designing a program to accomplish a behavioral objective for a low functioning student. The second and final step is to write out the behavior or stimulus-response chain that specifies how the objective will be accomplished by detailing all of the discriminative stimuli and responses that are involved.

Forward chaining

For the high functioning student who, as noted previously, already has the necessary responses in her behavioral repertoire, the behavioral objective can be reached through *forward chaining*. In forward chaining the responses are chained together beginning with the first response and ending with the last response which, of course, is followed by a reinforcer. (If one of the responses was not in the student's repertoire, it would first be shaped and then the sequence of behaviors would be chained together.) In the hair-shampooing example, walking to the sink would be reinforced first. Then walking to the sink and turning on the faucet would be chained together (required) before a reinforcer was given and so forth until the only response that was reinforced would be replacing the cap on the shampoo bottle. At that point the behavioral objective would have been met and the behavior chain completed.

> Forward chaining is a procedure in which the first response in a behavior chain is taught first and the last response is taught last.

Generally, normal individuals and high functioning retarded students can be taught to accomplish a behavioral objective through forward chaining. Often it is unnecessary to reinforce each response individually, since the entire behavior chain can be verbally described and demonstrated (see Chapter 8).

Backward chaining

What happens if the student doesn't have any of the necessary responses that the task analysis specifies? Here the reason for the difference between task analysis and behavior chains becomes clear. When a student, such as a profoundly retarded student, doesn't have the necessary behaviors in his behavioral repertoire, a *backward chaining* procedure is used to accomplish the behavioral objective. Thus, of the two procedures, backward chaining will be of more interest and use to you.

> Backward chaining is a procedure in which the last response in a behavior chain is taught first and the first response is taught last.

The success of the backward chaining procedure depends on the accurate specification of the stimulus-response or behavior chain because backward chaining involves teaching the last response in the chain first and working backwards so that the first response in the chain is taught last. We begin with the last response because it's closest to the terminal reinforcer and therefore it's the strongest response because it's always associated with the immediate delivery of the terminal reinforcer. (The terminal reinforcer is always a more powerful reinforcer than any of the conditioned reinforcers, the discriminative stimuli, that are a part of the behavioral chain.) Conversely, the first response is the weakest response because it's furthest away from the terminal reinforcer.

Let's now look at how backward chaining could be used to teach shampooing to a severely or profoundly retarded student. Backward chaining would be used because this type of student has none of the necessary behaviors associated with shampooing in her behavioral repertoire. The behavior chain for shampooing her hair is as follows:

(1) $S^D \longrightarrow$ (sink)

(2) $R \longrightarrow$ (walk to sink)

(3) $S^D \longrightarrow$ (faucet)

(4) $R \longrightarrow$ (turn on faucet)

(5) $S^D \longrightarrow$ (water running)

(6) $R \longrightarrow$ (wet hair under faucet)

(7) $S^D \longrightarrow$ (wet hair)

(8) $R \longrightarrow$ (pick up shampoo bottle)

(9) $S^D \rightarrow$ (10) $R \rightarrow$ (11) $S^D \rightarrow$ (12) $R \rightarrow$
(shampoo   (open cap of   (open bottle   (apply
bottle in   shampoo)   of shampoo)   shampoo
hand)   to hair)

(13) $S^D \rightarrow$ (14) $R \rightarrow$ (15) $S^D \rightarrow$ (16) $R \rightarrow$
(shampoo in   (work   (lather in   (rinse hair)
hair)   shampoo   hair)
         into lather)

(17) $S^D \rightarrow$ (18) $R \rightarrow$ (19) $S^D \rightarrow$ (20) $R \rightarrow$
(wet hair)   (pick up   (towel in   (dry hair)
         towel)   hand)

(21) $S^D \rightarrow$ (22) $R \rightarrow$ (23) $S^D \rightarrow$ (24) $R \rightarrow$
(wet towel)   (hang up   (open bottle   (replace cap
         towel)   of shampoo)   on shampoo
                                                     bottle)

S^{R+}
(praise from instructor, an edible, and a hug or pat)

The instructor uses backward chaining as follows.

Step 1   (24) $R \rightarrow$ S^{R+}
          (replace cap   (praise from instructor, an edible, and
          on shampoo   a hug or pat)
          bottle)

The instructor has the student replace the bottle cap and then reinforces her.

Step 2   (22) $R \rightarrow$ (23) $S^D \rightarrow$ (24) $R \rightarrow$ S^{R+}
          (hang up   (open bottle   (replace cap
          towel)   of shampoo)   on shampoo
                                             bottle)

The instructor has the student hang up the towel and replace the bottle cap, and then reinforces her.

Step 3   (20) $R \rightarrow$ (21) $S^D \rightarrow$ (22) $R \rightarrow$ (23) $S^D \rightarrow$
          (dry hair)   (wet towel)   (hang up   (open bottle
                                      towel)   of shampoo)

          (24) $R \rightarrow$ S^{R+}
          (replace cap
          on shampoo
          bottle)

The instructor has the student dry her hair, hang up the towel, and replace the bottle cap, and then reinforces her.

Step 4   (18) R $\longrightarrow$ (19) $S^D \longrightarrow$ (20) R $\longrightarrow$ (21) $S^D \longrightarrow$
           (pick up   (towel in   (dry hair)   (wet towel)
           towel)   hand)

          (22) R $\longrightarrow$ (23) $S^D \longrightarrow$ (24) R $\longrightarrow$ S^{R+}
           (hang up   (open bottle   (replace cap
           towel)   of shampoo) on sham-
                                      poo bottle)

The instructor has the student pick up the towel, dry her hair, hang up the towel, and replace the bottle cap, and then reinforces her.

Step 5   (16) R $\longrightarrow$ (17) $S^D \longrightarrow$ (18) R $\longrightarrow$ (19) $S^D \longrightarrow$
           (rinse hair) (wet hair)   (pick up   (towel in
                                  towel)   hand)

          (20) R $\longrightarrow$ (21) $S^D \longrightarrow$ (22) R $\longrightarrow$ (23) $S^D \longrightarrow$
           (dry hair)   (wet towel) (hang up   (open bottle
                                  towel)   of shampoo)

          (24) R $\longrightarrow$ S^{R+}
           (replace cap
           on shampoo
           bottle)

The instructor has the student rinse her hair, pick up the towel, dry her hair, hang up the towel, and replace the bottle cap, and then reinforces her.

Step 6   (14) R $\longrightarrow$ (15) $S^D \longrightarrow$ (16) R $\longrightarrow$ (17) $S^D \longrightarrow$
           (work   (lather in   (rinse hair) (wet hair)
           shampoo   hair)
           into lather)

          (18) R $\longrightarrow$ (19) $S^D \longrightarrow$ (20) R $\longrightarrow$ (21) $S^D \longrightarrow$
           (pick up   (towel in   (dry hair)   (wet towel)
           towel)   hand)

          (22) R $\longrightarrow$ (23) $S^D \longrightarrow$ (24) R $\longrightarrow$ S^{R+}
           (hang up   (open bottle (replace cap
           towel)   of shampoo) on shampoo
                                       bottle)

The instructor has the student work the shampoo into a lather, rinse her hair, pick up the towel, dry her hair, hang up the towel, and replace the bottle cap, and then reinforces her.

Step 7 (12) R →
(apply
shampoo
to hair)

(13) S^D →
(shampoo
in hair)

(14) R →
(work
shampoo
into lather)

(15) S^D →
(lather in
hair)

(16) R →
(rinse hair)

(17) S^D →
(wet hair)

(18) R →
(pick up
towel)

(19) S^D →
(towel in
hand)

(20) R →
(dry hair)

(21) S^D →
(wet towel)

(22) R →
(hang up
towel)

(23) S^D →
(open bottle
of shampoo)

(24) R →
(replace cap
on shampoo
bottle)

S^{R+}

The instructor has the student apply the shampoo, work the shampoo into a lather, rinse her hair, pick up the towel, dry her hair, hang up the towel, and replace the bottle cap, and then reinforces her.

Step 8 (10) R →
(open cap of
shampoo)

(11) S^D →
(open bottle
of shampoo)

(12) R →
(apply
shampoo
to hair)

(13) S^D →
(shampoo
in hair)

(14) R →
(work
shampoo
into lather)

(15) S^D →
(lather in
hair)

(16) R →
(rinse hair)

(17) S^D →
(wet hair)

(18) R →
(pick up
towel)

(19) S^D →
(towel in
hand)

(20) R →
(dry hair)

(21) S^D →
(wet towel)

(22) R →
(hang up
towel)

(23) S^D →
(open bottle
of shampoo)

(24) R →
(replace cap
on shampoo
bottle)

S^{R+}

The instructor has the student open the shampoo bottle, apply the shampoo, work the shampoo into a lather, rinse her hair, pick up the towel, dry her hair, hang up the towel, and replace the bottle cap, and then reinforces her.

Step 9 (8) $R \longrightarrow$ (9) $S^D \longrightarrow$ (10) $R \longrightarrow$ (11) $S^D \longrightarrow$
(pick up   (shampoo   (open cap of   (open bottle
shampoo   bottle in   shampoo)   of shampoo)
bottle)   hand)

(12) $R \longrightarrow$ (13) $S^D \longrightarrow$ (14) $R \longrightarrow$ (15) $S^D \longrightarrow$
(apply   (shampoo   (work   (lather in
shampoo   in hair)   shampoo   hair)
to hair)   into lather)

(16) $R \longrightarrow$ (17) $S^D \longrightarrow$ (18) $R \longrightarrow$ (19) $S^D \longrightarrow$
(rinse hair)   (wet hair)   (pick up   (towel in
     towel)   hand)

(20) $R \longrightarrow$ (21) $S^D \longrightarrow$ (22) $R \longrightarrow$ (23) $S^D \longrightarrow$
(dry hair)   (wet towel)   (hang up   (open bottle
     towel)   of shampoo)

(24) $R \longrightarrow$ S^{R+}
(replace cap
on shampoo
bottle)

The instructor has the student pick up the shampoo bottle, open the bottle, apply the shampoo, work the shampoo into a lather, rinse her hair, pick up the towel, dry her hair, hang up the towel, and replace the bottle cap, and then reinforces her.

Step 10 (6) $R \longrightarrow$ (7) $S^D \longrightarrow$ (8) $R \longrightarrow$ (9) $S^D \longrightarrow$
(wet hair   (wet hair)   (pick up   (shampoo
under   shampoo   bottle in
faucet)   bottle)   hand)

(10) $R \longrightarrow$ (11) $S^D \longrightarrow$ (12) $R \longrightarrow$ (13) $S^D \longrightarrow$
(open cap of   (open bottle   (apply   (shampoo
shampoo)   of shampoo)   shampoo   in hair)
     to hair)

(14) $R \longrightarrow$ (15) $S^D \longrightarrow$ (16) $R \longrightarrow$ (17) $S^D \longrightarrow$
(work   (lather in   (rinse hair)   (wet hair)
shampoo   hair)
into lather)

(18) R $\rightarrow$ (19) $S^D \rightarrow$ (20) R $\rightarrow$ (21) $S^D \rightarrow$
(pick up   (towel in   (dry hair)   (wet towel)
towel)   hand)

(22) R $\rightarrow$ (23) $S^D \rightarrow$ (24) R $\rightarrow$ S^{R+}
(hang up   (open bottle   (replace cap
towel)   of shampoo)   on shampoo
                                  bottle)

The instructor has the student wet her hair under the faucet, pick up the shampoo bottle, open the bottle, apply the shampoo, work the shampoo into a lather, rinse her hair, pick up the towel, dry her hair, hang up the towel, and replace the bottle cap, and then reinforces her.

Step 11 (4) R $\rightarrow$ (5) $S^D \rightarrow$ (6) R $\rightarrow$ (7) $S^D \rightarrow$
         (turn on   (water   (wet hair   (wet hair)
         faucet)   running)   under
                                             faucet)

         (8) R $\rightarrow$ (9) $S^D \rightarrow$ (10) R $\rightarrow$ (11) $S^D \rightarrow$
         (pick up   (shampoo   (open cap of   (open bottle
         shampoo   bottle   shampoo)   of shampoo)
         bottle)   in hand)

         (12) R $\rightarrow$ (13) $S^D \rightarrow$ (14) R $\rightarrow$ (15) $S^D \rightarrow$
         (apply   (shampoo   (work   (lather in
         shampoo   in hair)   shampoo   hair)
         to hair)   into lather)

         (16) R $\rightarrow$ (17) $S^D \rightarrow$ (18) R $\rightarrow$ (19) $S^D \rightarrow$
         (rinse hair)   (wet hair)   (pick up   (towel in
                                             towel)   hand)

         (20) R $\rightarrow$ (21) $S^D \rightarrow$ (22) R $\rightarrow$ (23) $S^D \rightarrow$
         (dry hair)   (wet towel)   (hang up   (open bottle
                                             towel)   of shampoo)

         (24) R $\rightarrow$ S^{R+}
         (replace cap
         on shampoo
         bottle)

The instructor has the student turn on the faucet, wet her hair, pick up the shampoo bottle, open the bottle, apply the shampoo, work the shampoo into a lather, rinse her hair, pick up the towel, dry her hair, hang up the towel, and replace the bottle cap, and then reinforces her.

Step 12 (2) R $\rightarrow$ (3) $S^D \rightarrow$ (4) R $\rightarrow$ (5) $S^D \rightarrow$
      (walk to   (faucet)   (turn on   (water
      sink)   faucet)   running)

      (6) R $\rightarrow$ (7) $S^D \rightarrow$ (8) R $\rightarrow$ (9) $S^D \rightarrow$
      (wet hair   (wet hair)   (pick up   (shampoo
      under   shampoo   bottle in
      faucet)   bottle)   hand)

      (10) R $\rightarrow$ (11) $S^D \rightarrow$ (12) R $\rightarrow$ (13) $S^D \rightarrow$
      (open cap of (open bottle (apply   (shampoo
      shampoo)   of shampoo) shampoo   in hair)
                                   to hair)

      (14) R $\rightarrow$ (15) $S^D \rightarrow$ (16) R $\rightarrow$ (17) $S^D \rightarrow$
      (work   (lather in   (rinse hair) (wet hair)
      shampoo   hair)
      into lather)

      (18) R $\rightarrow$ (19) $S^D \rightarrow$ (20) R $\rightarrow$ (21) $S^D \rightarrow$
      (pick up   (towel in   (dry hair)   (wet towel)
      towel)   hand)

      (22) R $\rightarrow$ (23) $S^D \rightarrow$ (24) R $\rightarrow$ SR^+
      (hang up   (open bottle (replace cap
      towel)   of shampoo) on shampoo
                                  bottle)

The instructor has the student walk to the sink, turn on the faucet, wet her hair, pick up the shampoo bottle, open the bottle, apply the shampoo, work the shampoo into a lather, rinse her hair, pick up the towel, dry her hair, hang up the towel, and replace the bottle cap, and then reinforces her.

     The number of steps involved in using backward chaining to teach a task will vary according to the complexity of the task. If you have never used a backward chaining procedure before, begin using it with a very simple task that involves only a few steps or discriminative stimuli, such as eating with a spoon. Similarly, if your students have never been taught by backward chaining, pick a simple task involving few steps for their first exposure to the procedure. Following this simple rule will increase the chances of success for both you and your students.

Here's another example of backward chaining. In this case, a student will be taught how to pull his pants up from his ankles. The response chain (task analysis) is as follows: The student will

Step 1 Reach for his pants
Step 2 Grasp his pants
Step 3 Pull his pants up to his calves
Step 4 Pull his pants to his knees
Step 5 Pull his pants to his thighs
Step 6 Pull his pants over his buttocks
Step 7 Pull his pants to his waist

The backward chaining sequence for this task would be as follows.

Step 1 The teacher puts the pants on the student so that they are just 1 to 2 inches below his waist. She then points to his pants, says, "Pants up," and guides his hands to the waistband of his pants. The student only needs to raise his pants 1 to 2 inches to receive the reinforcer.

Step 2 The student's pants are put on him so that they are just below his buttocks. A gestural prompt (pointing to his pants) and verbal prompt ("Pants up") are given and the physical prompt (guiding the student's hands to the waistband) is faded. The student receives a reinforcer when his pants are raised to his waist.

Step 3 The student's pants are put on him so that they are resting on his thighs. When the student responds successfully to the verbal and gestural prompts by raising his pants to his waist, he is reinforced.

Step 4 The student's pants are at his knees. When he raises his pants to his waist following the gestural prompt (the verbal prompt is faded), he is reinforced.

Step 5 The student's pants are at his calves. When he raises his pants to his waist following the gestural prompt, he is reinforced.

Step 6 The student's pants are at his ankles. When he raises his pants to his waist following the gestural prompt, he is reinforced.

In this example and whenever you use backward chaining, keep in mind that you also will use prompting, fading, shaping, and reinforcement.

The advantages of using backward chaining to teach a complex sequence of behaviors that is not in the student's behavioral repertoire are

1. The response closest to the terminal reinforcer is taught first. This is very important because it ensures that the student will be successful at the beginning of training since he only has to make one simple response in order to be reinforced.

2. The task (chain or sequence) is broken down into the smallest possible steps (responses) so that the student should be capable of learning the response chain. When a backward chaining procedure fails to teach a student, it's not because the student can't learn; rather, it's because the task has not been broken down into its simplest and most elementary components.

There are a few disadvantages associated with the use of backward chaining. They will be discussed in the next chapter when backward chaining and graduated guidance are compared and contrasted as techniques for teaching a complex sequence of behaviors.

The following techniques will help you use backward chaining effectively:

1. Use auxiliary discriminative stimuli (S^Ds) in addition to the S^Ds that are an integral part of the behavior chain. The auxiliary S^Ds are prompts such as instructions, gestures, and physical guidance. For example, in teaching pants raising, the instructor pointed to the pants, said "Pants up," and guided the student's hands to the waistband (Step 1).

2. Combine imitative prompts with the backward chaining. In teaching pants raising, the instructor could have worn a large pair of pants and demonstrated (modeled) the chain or various steps in pants raising while the student was watching.

3. Combine fading with the backward chaining. As an example, the verbal prompt was faded in Step 4 of teaching pants raising.

4. Combine shaping with the backward chaining. During the initial teaching of pants raising (Step 1) the instructor might have to reinforce a slight upward tug of the waistband.

5. Use continuous reinforcement in the beginning and only switch to intermittent reinforcement when the student has successfully performed the chain over several trials.

Practice Set 9B

Answers the following questions.

1. Here is a behavior (stimulus-response) chain of eating with a spoon. Label the responses (Rs), discriminative stimuli (S^Ds), and terminal reinforcers (S^{R+}s).

| (spoon beside plate of food) | (pick up spoon) | (spoon in hand) | (scoop food onto spoon) |

| (food on spoon) | (raise spoon toward mouth) | (spoon near mouth) | (place spoon in mouth) |

(food, praise)

2. In the previous chain, "spoon in hand" serves as a discriminative stimulus for which response and as a conditioned reinforcer for which response?

3. Assume that the student who was to be taught to eat with a spoon had all of the necessary self-feeding behaviors in his behavioral repertoire. Now write out the task analysis for accomplishing the behavioral objective of eating with a spoon. Would you use forward or backward chaining in order to accomplish the objective?

4. Suppose that the student who was to be taught self-feeding had all the necessary behaviors in his behavioral repertoire except for picking up the spoon. How would you add this new behavior to his repertoire?

5. Suppose that the student who was to be taught self-feeding had none of the necessary behaviors in his behavioral repertoire. What technique would you use to teach him self-feeding? How would you go about employing that technique?

6. The two advantages of backward chaining are (a) the r_____ closest to the t_____ reinforcer is taught first and (b) the task is broken down into the smallest possible s_____.

7. Normal individuals and high functioning retarded students typically learn a complex series of behaviors through f_____ chaining, whereas severely retarded students usually require b_____ chaining.

8. The five techniques that can be combined with backward chaining to make it more effective are (a) p_____ (or the use of supplemental S^Ds), (b) using i_____ prompts, (c) f_____, (d) s_____, and (e) using c_____ r_____ in the beginning.

The answers are on page 202.

ENTRY BEHAVIORS

Once you have developed a detailed list of sequenced steps that must be performed to accomplish the objective, you are ready to determine the final task analysis component: the student's *entry behaviors*. In effect, a student's entry behaviors are what she can do before we give her any instruction.

> Entry behaviors are those behaviors that the student possesses before instruction begins.

To determine the student's entry behaviors, or current level of performance, you review the sequence of steps to see if the student can perform any of them. There are several sources of information that will aid your review: (1) past written records of her behavior, (2) conversations with her parents or former teachers and caretakers, and (3) current observations of her behavior. You should rely primarily on your *own* direct observations of her behavior, since you may have no way to verify the reports of others. If you have been working closely with the student, you probably already have a good idea of what she can do. However, it is always best to double-check by setting up a situation in which you verify what she can do by providing her with the opportunity to complete the objective.

COMPLETE TASK ANALYSES

In summary, when conducting a complete task analysis, you do the following:

1. Specify the behavioral objective.
2. List the sequence of steps (behaviors) necessary to accomplish the objective.
3. Specify the student's entry behaviors.

The following example illustrates how these three factors are used to conduct a task analysis. Kevin's teacher has written the following behavioral objective: Kevin will feed himself with a spoon without the need for physical guidance and will complete his meal within 20 minutes. The teacher has written out the following sequence of steps necessary to accomplish the objective:

Step 1 Picks up spoon

Step 2 Scoops food into spoon

Step 3 Lifts spoon to mouth

Step 4 Places spoon in mouth

Step 5 Removes spoon from mouth

Step 6 Eats food

Step 7 Returns spoon to plate to begin next scoop

The teacher has observed Kevin at several meals and has seen him pick up the spoon and scoop food. However, Kevin has never lifted the spoon to his mouth but rather has waited for an instructor to walk over and physically guide him in eating. The teacher also knows, through observation, that Kevin has no motor problems, which means that there is no physiological reason for his reluctance to feed himself. Thus, the task analysis indicates that Kevin's entry behaviors are at Step 2 (he can do Steps 1 and 2) and that instruction should begin at Step 3.

Practice Set 9C

Certain critical information has been omitted from the following task analyses. Fill in the missing information.

I. 1. *Specify the behavioral objective:* During dressing training, the student will put on his pants when instructed to do so on 9 out of 10 trials.

    2. *List the sequence of steps necessary to accomplish the objective:* When handed his pants and instructed to put them on, the student will

    Step 1 Reach for his pants

    Step 2 Sit down

    Step 3 Put his feet through the appropriate pants leg openings

    Step 4 Pull pants over ankles

    Step 5 Stand up

    Step 6 Pull his pants up to his c_____

    Step 7 Pull his pants up to his hips

    Step 8 _____ buttocks

    Step 9 Pull his pants up to his waist

    3. *Specify the student's entry behaviors:* The student can put his feet through the appropriate pants leg openings.

    Instruction should begin at Step _____.

II. 1. *Specify the behavioral objective:* During dressing training, the student will fold her socks correctly when instructed to do so on 9 out of 10 trials.

    2. *List the sequence of steps necessary to accomplish the objective:* The student will

Step 1 Take socks from instructor and place them on a table

Step 2 Place one sock on top of the other, heel to heel, toe to toe

Step 3 Roll socks from the toes to the tops

Step 4 Spread open the end of the sock on the outside of the roll

Step 5 Tuck inside of roll into the open end of outer sock

3. *Specify the student's entry behaviors:* The student can place one sock on top of the other.

Instruction should begin at Step _____.

III. 1. *Specify the behavioral objective:* During personal hygiene training, the student will shampoo her hair when handed a bottle of shampoo without instruction.

2. *List the sequence of steps necessary to accomplish the objective:* The student will

Step 1   Take the bottle of shampoo

Step 2   _____ shampoo bottle cap

Step 3   Set cap down

Step 4   Pour shampoo in one hand

Step 5   Set bottle down

Step 6   Apply shampoo to hair

Step 7   Work shampoo into a _____

Step 8   Turn on water

Step 9   Rinse hair

Step 10 Turn off water

Step 11 Replace cap on shampoo bottle

Step 12 _____ with towel

3. *Specify the student's entry behaviors:* The student can apply shampoo to her hair.

Instruction should begin at Step _____.

IV. 1. *Specify the behavioral objective:* During fine motor training, the student will independently close a snap on a pair of pants on three out of four trials when instructed to do so.

2. *List the sequence of steps necessary to accomplish the objective:* The student will

Step 1 Grasp the right side of the waistband with his right thumb behind the snap and his right forefinger near the front of the snap

Step 2 Grasp the left side of the waistband with his left forefinger over the outside of the snap and his left thumb behind the waistband and near the snap

Step 3 Move the snaps together so that the top of the snap is resting on the bottom of the snap

Step 4 Exert pressure with his right thumb and left forefinger so that the snap closes

3. *Specify the student's entry behaviors:* The student can grasp a pair of pants at the waistband.

Instruction should begin at Step _____.

V. 1. *Specify the behavioral objective:* When instructed and with physical guidance from the instructor, the student will clap her hands on 8 out of 10 trials.

2. *List the sequence of steps necessary to accomplish the objective:* The student will

Step 1 Allow the instructor to hold her hands

Step 2 Allow the instructor to move her hands forward when she is told "Clap"

Step 3 Allow the instructor to clap her hands together

3. *Specify the student's entry behaviors:* The student allows the instructor to hold her hands.

Instruction should begin at Step _____.

VI. You would like a student to wet his toothbrush without help when instructed to do so at a 90% accuracy level.

1. *Specify the behavioral objective:* _____

_____

2. *List the sequence of steps necessary to accomplish the objective:* The student will

Step 1 _____

Step 2 Pick up his toothbrush

Step 3 Place the toothbrush under the water

Step 4 _____

3. *Specify the student's entry behaviors:* The student can turn water on and off.

Instruction should begin at Step _____.

The answers are on pages 202 and 203.

Obviously, a task analysis must be individualized for each student, since each differs according to her entry behaviors, whether or not she requires physical guidance, and other considerations. Thus, the number of required steps will differ for each student. In this chapter you have received only a brief introduction to task analysis. For more information, please refer to the publications listed in the Suggested Readings section at the end of the chapter.

SUMMARY

The task analysis model is used to determine what behaviors a student needs to be taught to accomplish an objective. A task analysis has three main components: a description of the behavioral objective or goal, a detailed description of each behavior or step needed to accomplish the objective, and an assessment of the student's entry behavior or current ability level. To conduct a task analysis, begin by specifying the objective, then list *in order* each step in the sequence of behaviors needed to accomplish the objective. Listing the sequence of steps in the task can be done from memory or by physically performing each behavior in the sequence. The method to be used can be determined by answering three questions: (1) Are you familiar with the objective? (2) Is there a likelihood that you might omit a step or crucial detail? (3) Is any special equipment or area needed?

Most of our behavior occurs in the form of stimulus-response or behavior chains that consist of a series of discriminative stimuli and responses that ends with a terminal reinforcer. A discriminative stimulus in a behavior chain serves as a conditioned reinforcer for the response it follows and as a discriminative stimulus for the response it precedes.

A task analysis is simply the specification of the responses in a behavior chain that must be performed in order to reach the behavioral objective. Thus, the behavioral objective in a task analysis is the completion of the behavior chain. When a task analysis is used, the behavioral objective is accomplished through forward chaining because the responses are taught from the beginning of the chain. Forward chaining is used when a student has the necessary responses in her behavioral repertoire so that all that must be done is to chain the responses together. Generally, forward chaining is not an appropriate procedure to use with severely and profoundly retarded students.

Backward chaining is used to teach a behavior chain when the student has few, if any, of the necessary responses in her behavioral repertoire. In backward chaining, the last response in the chain is taught first and the first response in the chain is taught last because the last response is closest to the terminal reinforcer. This is an advantage of backward chaining because it increases the likelihood that the student will be successful. A second advantage of backward chaining is that it breaks the task (chain or sequence) into small, easily mastered steps. Five ways to maximize the use of backward chaining are to (1) use auxiliary discriminative stimuli (prompts), (2) add imitative prompts, (3) combine fading with the backward chaining, (4) combine shaping with the backward chaining, and (5) use continuous reinforcement when the chain is first being taught.

To finish the task analysis, you need to assess the student's entry behavior. The sequence of steps should be reviewed to determine which ones the student already can perform. Several sources of information on the student's performance are (1) past records of her behavior, (2) conversations with her parents or former teachers and caretakers, and (3) direct observations of her behavior, which is undoubtedly the most reliable source of information.

SUGGESTED READINGS

Cronin, K. A., & Cuvo, A. J. Teaching mending skills to mentally retarded adolescents. *Journal of Applied Behavior Analysis*, 1979, *12*, 401-406.

Foxx, R. M., & Azrin, N. H. *Toilet training the retarded: A rapid program for day and nighttime independent toileting.* Champaign, Ill.: Research Press, 1973.

Gold, M. W. Stimulus factors in skill training of the retarded on a complex assembly task: Acquisition, transfer, and retention. *American Journal of Mental Deficiency*, 1972, *76*, 517-526.

Horner, R. D., & Keilitz, I. Training mentally retarded adolescents to brush their teeth. *Journal of Applied Behavior Analysis*, 1975, *8*, 301-309.

Mager, R. F., & Pipe, P. *Analyzing performance problems or "You really oughta wanna."* Belmont, Calif.: Fearon Pitman Publishers, 1970.

Mechner, F. Science education and behavioral technology. In R. Glaser (Ed.), *Teaching machines and programmed learning.* Washington, D.C.: National Education Association, 1965.

Walls, R. T., Zane, T., & Ellis, W. D. Forward chaining, backward chaining, and whole-task methods: Training assembly tasks in vocational rehabilitation. *Behavior Modification*, 1981, *5*, 61-74.

Walls, R. T., Zane, T., & Thvedt, J. E. Trainers' personal methods compared to two structured training strategies. *American Journal of Mental Deficiency*, 1980, *84*, 495-507.

Weisberg, P. Operant procedures with the retardate. In N. R. Ellis (Ed.), *International review of research in mental retardation* (Vol. 5). New York: Academic Press, 1971.

Weiss, K. M. A comparison of forward and backward procedures for the acquisition of response chains in humans. *Journal of the Experimental Analysis of Behavior*, 1978, *29*, 255-259.

Review Set 9

1. The first step in performing a task analysis is to specify the b_____ objective.

2. The next step is to determine the s_____ of steps needed to accomplish the objective.

3. The final step is to determine the student's e_____ behavior(s).

4. A b_____ c_____ is a sequence of stimuli and responses that ends with a terminal reinforcer.

5. A behavior chain is also known as a s_____ -r_____ chain.

6. The reinforcer that comes at the end of a behavior chain is called the t_____ reinforcer.

7. A stimulus that is associated with reinforcement is called a c_____ reinforcer.

8. A d_____ stimulus is associated with reinforcement.

9. A d_____ s_____ in a behavior chain has a dual role. It serves as a d_____ s_____ for the response it precedes and as a c_____ r_____ for the response it follows.

10. The abbreviation for discriminative stimulus is _____.

11. The abbreviation for a conditioned reinforcer is _____.

12. The abbreviation for terminal reinforcer is _____.

13. A task analysis is nothing more than a specification of the r_____ in a behavior chain that must be performed in order to reach the behavioral objective.

14. F_____ c_____ is used to accomplish a behavioral objective when the student has all the necessary behaviors in the behavior chain in her b_____ r_____.

15. Forward chaining is teaching the f_____ response in the chain first and teaching the l_____ response in the chain last.

16. When the student does not have the necessary behaviors in her behavioral repertoire, she should be taught a behavior chain using b_____ c_____.

17. In backward chaining, the l_____ response in the chain is taught first and the f_____ response in the chain is taught last.

18. After the sequence of steps for attaining an objective is decided upon, it should be reviewed to determine which ones the student can p_____.

19. Several sources of information on a student's performance are (a) past r_____ of behavior, (b) c_____ with parents or former teachers and caretakers, and (c) d_____ o_____ of the student's behavior, which is the most reliable source.

Answers are found on page 203.

CHAPTER 10

Graduated Guidance

Now that you've learned to use backward and forward chaining, we can introduce a technique developed by the author that should be particularly helpful in teaching your severely and profoundly retarded students. It is called *graduated guidance*. In this chapter you'll learn the three parts of this technique and how to use them in training. The disadvantages of backward chaining and the advantages of graduated guidance also will be compared.

> Graduated guidance is a technique combining physical guidance and fading in which the physical guidance is systematically and gradually reduced and then faded completely.

Graduated guidance is used to teach a behavior chain through forward chaining. It represents a radical departure from backward chaining because the entire behavior chain is completed each time graduated guidance is used. Graduated guidance is especially useful for students whose intellectual deficits make it difficult for them to understand simple verbal and gestural prompts and/or for students who require a lot of physical prompting. The major difference between graduated guidance and manual guidance (as in physical prompting) is that in graduated guidance the amount of the instructor's physical guidance (hand pressure) is adjusted from moment to moment depending on the student's performance (behavior) at that moment.

THE COMPONENTS OF GRADUATED GUIDANCE

There are three parts to the graduated guidance technique: full graduated guidance, partial graduated guidance, and

129

shadowing. These three parts reflect the amount of trainer participation in the student's performance of a particular sequence of behaviors. One part or all parts may be used during any training session. Graduated guidance is used as follows:*

1. Exert no more force at any given moment than is needed to move the student's hand in the desired direction.
2. At the start of each trial, use the minimal force (even a touch) and build up until the hand starts moving.
3. Once the hand starts to move, decrease the guidance instantly and gradually as long as the guided hand continues to move.
4. If movement stops during a trial, increase the guiding force instantly and gradually to the point where movement again results.
5. If the guided hand pushes against you in the direction away from the proper motion, apply just enough force to counteract that force, thereby keeping the resisting hand in a nonmoving position.
6. As soon as the resisting hand decreases the degree of opposing force, instantly decrease the amount of force so that the student's resistance is again just being counterbalanced.
7. When the guided hand stops actively resisting, immediately but gradually start again to use just enough force to move the guided hand.
8. Once a trial starts, continue to guide the hand until the response is completed; do not give up or interrupt before the final step.
9. At the end of the trial, give a reinforcer.
10. The reinforcer should be given together with the desired physical effect produced by the completion of the response.
11. When the reinforcer is about to be given at the completion of the response, eliminate the guidance by withdrawing even touch contact and then give the reinforcer.
12. Verbal praise should also be given during the guidance but only at those moments when the student is actively participating in the movement and never while he is resisting or completely passive.

---

*Adapted with permission from *Toilet training the retarded: A rapid program for day and nighttime independent toileting* by R. M. Foxx and N. H. Azrin. Champaign, Ill.: Research Press, 1973, pp. 37-38.

During full graduated guidance, the instructor keeps her hands in full contact with the student's hands. She praises the student continuously as long as the student is moving his hands willingly in the desired direction. Let's look at an example of the use of graduated guidance to teach a student to pull his pants up from his ankles.

The instructor begins with *full graduated guidance*. She puts the pants on the student so that they are at his ankles. She then says, "Pants up" and guides the student's hands to the waistband of his pants. The instructor begins guiding the student's hands in raising his pants to his waist. As the pants are being raised, she praises him whenever he makes the slightest effort to raise the pants himself. The instructor keeps her hands on the student's hands throughout the training trial, from the beginning of the verbal prompt "Pants up" until the pants are raised to his waist. At this point an edible and a social reinforcer are given. If the student should resist the graduated guidance, the instructor would use just enough force to counteract the student's resistance and reduce and then eliminate this force when the student ceased resisting.

Once the student allows his hands to be guided without any resistance, the instructor begins using *partial graduated guidance*. During the partial graduated guidance, the instructor merely guides the student's hands with her thumb and forefinger. In this way the instructor fades the amount of physical contact so that the student takes more responsibility for raising his pants. She continues to praise all of the student's efforts to raise his pants, as well as when he allows her to use the partial graduated guidance, saying something such as "That's good, you're raising your pants. Good, keep raising your pants. Keep going. Good, pants up. Good."

When the student reliably raises his pants in response to the instructor's use of partial graduated guidance, the instructor begins using *shadowing*. During shadowing the instructor keeps her hands within an inch of the student's hands throughout the pants raising trial. If the student stops raising his pants at any time during the trial, the instructor reapplies partial or full graduated guidance (depending on which is necessary to motivate the student to perform the desired action) until the student once again begins raising his pants; at that point the instructor resumes the shadowing. As before, generous amounts of praise are given whenever the student is raising his pants. The use of shadowing permits the instructor to fade her physical contact so that it no longer serves as a physical prompt. In this way the student begins to attend only to the instructor's verbal prompts.

Within each training trial you can use all three parts of the graduated guidance technique. Your choice of whether to use full graduated guidance, partial graduated guidance, or shadowing depends on what the student is doing at the moment. For example, you might begin the pants raising trial using full graduated guidance, then switch to partial graduated guidance as the student begins taking over some of the pants raising action, and then begin shadowing when the student is raising his pants himself. If the student should stop the pants raising action at any time, guidance would be reapplied (either full or partial, whichever was necessary) until the student resumed the action, at which time you would resume the shadowing. Praise would be given throughout as long as the student was performing some appropriate pants raising action. For any instances of resistance, you would use only the amount of hand force necessary to counterbalance the resistive action.

Over time you'll eliminate the full graduated guidance, then the partial guidance, until you only need to shadow the student's hands during the activity. When only shadowing is necessary throughout a training trial, you'll begin to fade the shadowing by moving your hands further and further away from the student's hands. This fading should be done by moving your hands 2 inches from the student's hands on one trial, then 3 inches away on the next trial, and so forth, until you are approximately 2 feet away from the student. At that point the student should be performing the requested behavioral chain (here, pants raising) in response to just your verbal prompt or instruction ("Pants up"). Of course, you would reapply guidance (either partial or full) should the student stop somewhere along the chain. However, this is rarely necessary, since the student will have had a long history of performing the chain (raising his pants) and receiving reinforcers. Once you have faded yourself to the point where you are 2 feet away from the student, you should begin reducing the amount of praise that you give during the student's performance of the chain. This shouldn't be difficult since the student will be performing the chain rapidly. It's advisable to systematically reduce your praise over trials so that you ultimately only praise the student at the end of the chain.

A COMPARISON OF BACKWARD CHAINING
AND GRADUATED GUIDANCE

In Chapter 9 it was stated that the two advantages of backward chaining were that the response closest to the terminal reinforcer was taught first and that the task (or chain) was broken down into easily mastered steps. There are, however, two disadvantages of backward chaining:

1. You must wait for the student to respond. No matter what step the student is on or how small that step is, no reinforcement can be provided until the student performs the step. Thus, some training time is lost while you are waiting for the student to respond.

2. You can't provide any within-trial reinforcement because you must wait for the student to complete the trial before you deliver the reinforcement and praise.

These disadvantages of backward chaining result from the fact that each step (response) in the chain represents a discrete trial. Thus, any backward chaining program consists of many discrete trials as each response (step) is added to the chain.

The use of graduated guidance eliminates these two disadvantages of backward chaining because the entire chain is taught during each training trial. The only difference in each trial is the amount of physical guidance that is needed to ensure that the entire chain is completed.

Let's look at the two disadvantages of backward chaining and see how they are eliminated when graduated guidance is used. First, in graduated guidance, you don't need to wait for the student to respond (as with backward chaining). You are guiding the student in performing the behavior chain, which ensures that the student will always be successful in performing all the responses in the chain and that there will be no lost training time while waiting for the student to respond. Second, because the student is performing all of the responses in the chain during graduated guidance, you can provide within-trial reinforcement by constantly praising any of the student's efforts to perform the actions voluntarily. As a result you can use more reinforcement with graduated guidance than you can with backward chaining.

A final advantage of graduated guidance is that it incorporates *avoidance learning*, which is the learning that occurs when someone responds in order to avoid or escape something that is unpleasant to him. In the graduated guidance procedure, your physical guidance should serve as a mild irritant to the student. Eventually the student will learn to avoid the physical guidance by performing the requested chain or escape the ongoing physical guidance by beginning to perform the chain himself. Even the most retarded student is able to learn to avoid or escape the physical guidance because the guidance is reduced or terminated whenever the student responds appropriately. This reduction or elimination of the physical guidance on a moment-to-moment basis thus serves as a source of constant feedback to the student. In effect, the graduated guidance procedure offers you an ideal situation: the student responds to avoid the guidance, and his avoidance response is reinforced by a reduction or elimination of the guidance and by praise (social reinforcement) when he begins responding independently.

The advantages of graduated guidance are:

1. It doesn't require you to wait for the student to respond.
2. It allows within-trial reinforcement.
3. It incorporates avoidance learning.

Despite the obvious advantages of graduated guidance, there are two reasons why it might be advantageous for you to begin teaching your students with backward chaining. First, backward chaining requires less expertise than graduated guidance. Second, the use of backward chaining will help you understand and master task analysis and behavior chains because it requires you to identify the behavior chain and break it down into the smallest possible steps. Once you have gained expertise using backward chaining, you should be ready to begin using graduated guidance as well.

SUMMARY

Graduated guidance is a technique in which physical guidance and fading are combined such that the physical guidance is systematically and gradually reduced and then faded completely. Graduated guidance teaches a behavior chain through forward chaining and is especially useful for students who do not respond to simple verbal and gestural prompts or for whom a great deal of physical prompting is necessary. The three parts of graduated guidance are full graduated guidance, partial graduated guidance, and shadowing. In full guidance, your hands are on the student's hands throughout the trial; in partial guidance, you guide the student's hands with your thumb and forefinger; and in shadowing, you keep your hands within an inch of the student's hands. All three parts can be used in any one trial. Over time, both physical prompts and verbal reinforcement are faded.

Although backward chaining also is used to teach students, it has two disadvantages: (1) you must wait for the student to respond and thus lose some training time and (2) you cannot provide within-trial reinforcement. Graduated guidance eliminates these disadvantages because the entire chain is taught during each trial. The three advantages of graduated guidance are that (1) you don't have to wait for the student to respond, (2) within-trial reinforcement is possible, and (3) it incorporates avoidance learning. Avoidance learning plays an important role in graduated guidance because the student learns to respond appropriately (perform the behavior chain) in order to avoid or escape your physical guidance.

You should begin teaching your students using backward chaining. Once you have acquired sufficient expertise in the use of backward chaining, you can begin trying the graduated guidance procedure as a means of teaching the students complex skills.

SUGGESTED READINGS

Foxx, R. M. Developing overcorrection procedures for problem behaviors: A strategy for individualizing treatment programs. *8th Annual Meeting and Conference of the National Society for Autistic Children* (Proceedings), 1976, 102-134.

Foxx, R. M. Increasing a mildly retarded woman's attendance at self-help classes by overcorrection and instruction. *Behavior Therapy*, 1976, *7*, 390-396.

Foxx, R. M. The use of overcorrection to eliminate the public disrobing (stripping) of retarded women. *Behaviour Research and Therapy*, 1976, *14*, 53-61.

Foxx, R. M. Attention training: The use of overcorrection avoidance to increase the eye contact of autistic and retarded children. *Journal of Applied Behavior Analysis*, 1977, *10*, 489-499.

Foxx, R. M., & Azrin, N. H. The elimination of autistic self-stimulatory behavior by overcorrection. *Journal of Applied Behavior Analysis*, 1973, *6*, 1-14.

Foxx, R. M., & Azrin, N. H. *Toilet training the retarded: A rapid program for day and nighttime independent toileting.* Champaign, Ill.: Research Press, 1973.

Review Set 10

1. G_____ g_____ is a technique in which physical guidance and fading are combined to teach a behavior chain through forward chaining.

2. The three parts of graduated guidance are f_____ graduated guidance, p_____ graduated guidance, and s_____.

3. Graduated guidance is especially useful for students whose intellectual deficits make it difficult for them to understand simple v_____ and gestural prompts and/or for students who require a lot of p_____ prompting.

4. The major difference between manual guidance and graduated guidance is that with graduated guidance the amount of the instructor's physical guidance (hand pressure) is adjusted from m_____ to m_____ depending on the student's performance at that moment.

5. During full graduated guidance, the instructor keeps her hands in f_____ contact with the student's hands.

6. During partial graduated guidance, the instructor merely guides the student's hands with her t_____ and f_____.

7. During s_____, the instructor keeps her hands within an inch of the student's hands.

8. All three parts of graduated guidance can be used within each training t_____.

9. When the student resists the graduated guidance, the instructor uses just enough f_____ to counteract the student's resistance and then reduces and finally eliminates this f_____ as the student stops resisting.

10. P_____ is given throughout the graduated guidance so long as the student is performing some action appropriately.

11. When you have faded your presence to a point where you are 2 feet away from the student, you should begin reducing your praise until you only praise the student at the e_____ of the trial.

12. The two disadvantages of backward chaining are that (a) you must wait for the student to r_____ and (b) you cannot provide within-t_____ reinforcement.

13. The three advantages of graduated guidance are that (a) you don't have to wait for the student to r_____, (b) w_____-trial reinforcement is possible, and (c) it incorporates a_____ learning.

14. Avoidance learning occurs when the student learns to respond in order to a_____ or e_____ an unpleasant event.

15. In graduated guidance, the unpleasant event that leads to avoidance learning is the instructor's p_____ g_____.

16. You should teach your students using b_____
    c_____ until you have enough expertise to try grad-
    uated guidance.

The answers are on page 204.

CHAPTER 11

Baseline Measurement

In the preceding chapters you've learned how to design programs for your students. Now we'll discuss assessing behaviors to see if instruction is needed or if your instructional programs are effective. In this chapter you'll learn how to measure the natural occurrence of a target behavior, using one of two methods, and how to decide when enough measurement has been done for instruction to begin.

Measurement of a naturally occurring behavior reveals its *operant level.*

> The operant level is a description of the frequency of a behavior before instruction begins.

An operant level tells you how often the behavior occurs before you attempt to increase it. For example, Mr. Weir would like to develop a program to increase the number of foods that Mickey, an autistic youngster, will eat. Before beginning the program, Mr. Weir should determine how many different foods Mickey presently will eat. Mr. Weir will use this information to determine the effectiveness of the program by simply comparing the number of foods Mickey eats prior to training versus the number he eats after training. The period of time during which Mickey's eating behavior is measured before the intervention is called the *baseline period.*

> A baseline is the period of time during which a behavior is observed and measured without any intervention (training).

Determining the operant level during a baseline condition provides an objective measurement of the behavior's occurrence and helps in evaluating the effectiveness of a training program. It's extremely important that we know how often the behavior occurs under natural conditions so that we can make intelligent decisions about how to increase it. Otherwise we find ourselves using impressions or guesses concerning the student's behavior, rather than using a scientifically based teaching model.

Often it will appear that a behavior occurs more often than it really does. For example, Dr. Martin, the consulting psychologist, believes that there is no need to design a program to increase Fred's eye contact because every time he encounters Fred, Fred is looking at him. However, Fred's teacher, Ms. Wright, insists that there is a problem with Fred's eye contact because he rarely looks at her or her aide when instructed to do so. To resolve the question, Dr. Martin and Ms. Wright decide to conduct a 2-week baseline in order to determine Fred's operant level of eye contact. The baseline reveals that Fred only exhibited eye contact every few days except when Dr. Martin entered the classroom. On those occasions Fred always looked at Dr. Martin, perhaps because he was a novel stimulus since he only visited the classroom once a week. Measuring the occurrence of the behavior (operant level) during a baseline demonstrated to Dr. Martin that Fred's eye contact was a problem, as Ms. Wright had suggested. As a result Dr. Martin helped Ms. Wright design an eye contact training program to use with Fred.

Determining the operant level during baseline also helps us to establish whether or not our teaching program has been effective. Mr. Rose's behavioral objective was to train Willie to pull his pants up from his ankles. When he tallied Willie's operant level of pulling up his pants, he found that Willie could pull his pants up from his thighs (Mr. Rose was using a backward chaining procedure, as discussed in Chapter 9), and would do so only twice during each 10-minute training session. A week after giving Willie daily instructional sessions in pants raising, Mr. Rose's data revealed that Willie could still only pull his pants up from his thighs and would do so only twice during each session. Willie's pants raising behavior had not increased during the training, nor had he learned any more of the behavior chain of pants raising (e.g., raising his pants from his knees). As a result, Mr. Rose knew he needed to reevaluate his training techniques, his task analysis, and his use of reinforcers before attempting any further training with Willie.

TAKING A BASELINE

Determining an operant level of behavior by taking a baseline measurement can be accomplished in a variety of ways depending on the particular behavior you wish to measure. We'll consider two common ways: frequency counting and time sampling.

Frequency Counting

> Frequency counting is a recording method in which the number of times a behavior occurs during a specified period of time is tallied.

The first and most general method is *frequency counting*, in which you tally the number of times the behavior occurs during a specified period of time. Each time the behavior occurs, simply place a hatch mark (/) or check mark (✔) on a sheet of paper. For example, you may wish to determine how often your student, Mary Kelly, will independently feed herself with a spoon during lunch.

Name: Mary Kelly
Behavior to Be Counted: Number of times Mary independently places a spoonful of food in her mouth during lunch

Date	Number of Times Behavior Occurred	Recorder
August 1	✔ ✔	Spear
August 2	✔ ✔	Spear
August 3	✔ ✔ ✔ ✔ ✔	Spear
August 4	✔ ✔ ✔	Essex
August 5	✔ ✔ ✔	Spear

The baseline record reveals that Mary's operant level of self-feeding ranged from two to five times per lunch and averaged three times.

Time Sampling

> Time sampling is a recording method in which the student is observed at fixed intervals for a specified period of time and the occurrence or absence of a behavior during each interval is recorded.

A second common method of determining the operant level is *time sampling.* In time sampling you simply observe the student at fixed intervals, such as every 5 minutes, for a specified period of time, such as 30 seconds, and then record whether or not the behavior occurred. The behavior can then be expressed as a percentage, that is, the number of instances or observations in which the behavior was observed divided by the number of observations, times 100.

$$\frac{\text{number of instances}}{\begin{array}{c}\text{number of possible}\\ \text{instances}\end{array}} \times 100 = \text{percentage of time behavior occurs}$$

Thus, rather than counting each occurrence of the behavior, you simply determine the percentage of time the behavior occurs. Time sampling is especially useful when the operant level of the behavior is very high, such as with self-stimulatory behavior, or when you wish to measure a behavior that may go on for several seconds or minutes, such as on-task behavior. The following examples illustrate the time sampling method of recording.

Billy Thomson appears to rock continuously throughout the day and his attendant has decided to determine his operant level of rocking during an hour period. The time sampling baseline record on August 1 shows that Billy was rocking in 76.9% of the observed intervals.

Name: Billy Thomson

Behavior to Be Measured: *Rocking.* Billy will be observed every 5 minutes for 15 seconds during a 1-hour period. A check mark indicates that he rocked at some time during the observation interval. A circle indicates that rocking did not occur during the observation interval.

Date: August 1		Recorded by: Ed Jones
Time	Rocking Occurred (✔)	No Rocking Occurred (0)
9:00	✔	
9:05	✔	
9:10	✔	
9:15	✔	
9:20	✔	
9:25		0
9:30	✔	
9:35	✔	
9:40		0
9:45		0

Time	Rocking Occurred (✔)	No Rocking Occurred (0)
9:50	✔	
9:55	✔	
10:00	✔	
Total	10	3

Percentage of Time Rocking = 76.9% (10 ÷ 13 x 100)

Bobby James' teachers are interested in determining his operant level of on-task behavior during his favorite activity of finger painting, which lasts for 15 minutes. The time sampling baseline record on June 3 shows that Bobby was on task during 62.5% of the observed intervals.

Name: Bobby James

Behavior to Be Measured: *On-task finger painting behavior.* Bobby will be observed every minute for 5 seconds during the 15-minute finger painting activity. A check mark indicates that he was finger painting (on task) at some time during the observation interval. A circle indicates that Bobby did not finger paint during the observation interval.

Date: June 3		Recorded by: Harvey Martin
Time	Finger Painting Occurred (✔)	No Finger Painting Occurred (0)
9:00	✔	
9:01	✔	
9:02	✔	
9:03	✔	
9:04	✔	
9:05		0
9:06	✔	
9:07	✔	
9:08		0
9:09		0
9:10	✔	
9:11	✔	
9:12	✔	
9:13		0
9:14		0
9:15		0
Total	10	6

Percentage of Time Finger Painting = 62.5% (10 ÷ 16 x 100)

ENDING THE BASELINE CONDITION

How do you determine how long to conduct baseline recordings? Let's return to the baseline record of Mary Kelly's self-feeding as an example.

Name: Mary Kelly
Behavior to Be Counted: Number of times Mary independently places a spoonful of food in her mouth during lunch

Date	Number of Times Behavior Occurred	Recorder
August 1	✔ ✔	Spear
August 2	✔ ✔	Spear
August 3	✔ ✔ ✔ ✔ ✔	Spear
August 4	✔ ✔ ✔	Essex
August 5	✔ ✔ ✔	Spear

The baseline record reveals that Mary's operant level of self-feeding ranged from two to five times per lunch and averaged three times. Note that the recording was conducted for 5 days. The number of days was not chosen arbitrarily. Rather, the baseline was conducted until the operant level appeared to be stable and the number for the final baseline day was no higher than the number for the previous day.

How do you know when you have a stable baseline? The answer comes from deciding whether or not the baseline adequately shows the range (variability) of the behavior or reveals any consistent upward trend. Thus, we determine when to cease baseline recording by asking two questions. First, does the baseline adequately show the range (variability) of the behavior? If the answer is yes, then we ask the second question: is the final baseline data point (number) as low or lower than the data point from the previous baseline session or day?

Let's consider these two questions in regard to Mary's baseline record of self-feeding.

1. *Does the baseline adequately show the range of the behavior?*
   In other words, was the baseline conducted over a long enough period of time to ensure that no drastic changes or fluctuations in the operant level occurred? Mary's operant level of self-feeding showed no drastic changes—she did not feed herself one time at lunch one day and nine times the following day. Rather, her self-feeding ranged between two and five times. Thus, the answer to the first question would be "Yes, the baseline accurately shows the range of the measured be-

havior." Because the answer is yes, it's appropriate to ask the second question. However, if the answer is no, then recording must be continued until you can answer yes.

2. *Is the final baseline data point as low or lower than the data point from the previous baseline session or day?* Mary fed herself with a spoon three times on the last day and three times on the previous day. Thus, the answer to the second question is also yes.

Since the answer to both questions is yes, baseline data no longer need to be recorded, and it's appropriate to begin a program to increase Mary's self-feeding. If the answer to either question had been no, baseline data would still have been collected until a yes could be given to both questions. Remember, don't pose the second question until the first is answered affirmatively.

As mentioned previously, determining the operant level by conducting a baseline condition helps you determine the effectiveness of a teaching or training program, since the level of the behavior during the program can be compared to the level during baseline. When you want to increase a behavior, then that behavior should be higher in the program condition than it was during baseline. If it is, we can say the program was effective. However, if the baseline is terminated prematurely and the behavior is increasing when the baseline is terminated, we have no sound way of evaluating whether or not the program is working. (In fact, it could be that no program was necessary.)

For instance, a major error would have been made if the teacher had decided to begin a program to increase Mary's self-feeding after the third day of recording. Mary had increased her self-feeding from two responses on August 2 to five responses on August 3. Had the program increased her self-feeding responses to seven on August 4, the argument could have been made that Mary was already beginning to increase her self-feeding independent of the program. As a result the teacher would never know whether or not the program was successful in increasing self-feeding or whether it simply coincided with the same day that Mary had increased her self-feeding. Because of this dilemma, the teacher would not be likely to use the program to teach self-feeding to other students. In effect, Mary's teacher would have failed to ask the two questions that would tell whether or not she could terminate the baseline recording.

Let's return to the baseline record of Bobby James' on-task behavior during a finger painting activity. Before, we only had Bobby's first day of baseline, whereas now we have a 5-day record.

Name: Bobby James

Behavior to Be Measured: *Percentage of time Bobby stays on task.* The task is finger painting. Bobby will be observed every minute for 5 seconds during the 15-minute finger painting activity each school day.

Date	Percent On Task	Recorder
June 3	62.5	Martin
June 4	52	Martin
June 5	60.5	Bornstein
June 6	58	Martin
June 7	58	Bornstein

The 5-day baseline record reveals that Bobby's operant level of on-task behavior ranged from 52 to 62.5% and averaged 58.2%. Is this baseline record sufficient to allow us to begin a program to increase Bobby's on-task behavior? The record shows that the baseline was stable, since it was conducted long enough to ensure that no drastic changes in the operant level occurred. Furthermore, the final baseline percentage was as low or lower than the previous session or day. As a result, we can suspend baseline recording and begin Bobby's treatment program.

Practice Set 11

Answer the following questions for each case.

1. Name: Susan Brown

   Behavior to Be Counted: Number of times Susan independently sits down in her seat when requested to do so

Date	Number of Times Behavior Occurred	Recorder
July 16	✔ ✔ ✔ ✔	Shelton
July 17	✔ ✔ ✔	Shelton
July 18	✔ ✔ ✔ ✔ ✔	Stevens
July 19	✔ ✔ ✔	Stevens
July 20	✔ ✔ ✔ ✔	Shelton

   a. The baseline record reveals that Susan's operant level of sitting when instructed ranged from _____ to _____ times per day and averaged _____ times per day.

   b. Was the baseline conducted long enough to ensure that no drastic changes in the operant level occurred?

   c. Was the final baseline data point as low or lower than the previous day?

   d. Are more baseline recordings required? Why or why not?

---

2. Name: Ross Hall

Behavior to Be Counted: Number of times Ross walks to an instructor when requested to do so

Date	Number of Times Behavior Occurred	Recorder
November 3	/	Ansel
November 4	/ /	Kohrs
November 5	0	Kohrs
November 6	/	Kohrs
November 7	/ /	Springer
November 10	/	Kohrs

   a. The baseline record reveals that Ross' operant level of walking to his instructor ranged from _____ to _____ times per day and averaged _____ times per day.

   b. Was the baseline conducted long enough to ensure that no drastic changes in the operant level occurred?

   c. Was the final baseline data point as low or lower than the previous day?

   d. Are more baseline recordings required? Why or why not?

---

3. Name: Eric LeRouge

Behavior to Be Measured: *Eric sitting in his chair.* Eric will be observed for 5 seconds every 5 minutes during a 1-hour period. A hatch mark indicates that he was in his chair during the observation interval. A circle indicates that Eric was out of his seat during the observation interval.

Date: September 6		Recorded by: Crystal Peters
Time	In Seat (/)	Out of Seat (0)
1:00	/	
1:05		0
1:10	/	
1:15	/	
1:20	/	
1:25		0
1:30		0
1:35		0

Time	In Seat (/)	Out of Seat (0)
1:40		0
1:45		0
1:50	/	
1:55		0
Total	5	7

What percentage of the time was Eric in his seat?

4. Name: Phil Hunter

Behavior to Be Measured: *Percentage of time Phil stays on task.* The task is coloring with a crayon. Phil will be observed every minute for 5 seconds during the 15-minute coloring session each school day.

Date	Percent On Task	Recorder
October 8	30	Barnes
October 9	35	Barnes
October 12	27	Bornstein
October 13	30	Barnes
October 14	24	Bornstein

a. The baseline record reveals that Phil's operant level of staying on task ranged from _____ to _____% per day and averaged _____%.

b. Was the baseline conducted long enough to ensure that no drastic changes in the operant level occurred?

c. Was the final baseline percentage as low or lower than the previous day?

d. Are more baseline data required? Why or why not?

5. Name: Pat Stephens

Behavior to Be Measured: *Percentage of time Pat is in her seat.* Pat will be observed for 10 seconds every 5 minutes throughout the 6-hour school day and her percentage of in-seat behavior will be calculated for each hourly session.

Date: November 11

Hour Number	Percent In Seat	Recorder
1	10	Smithwick
2	37	Smithwick
3	68	Littlejohn
4	21	Littlejohn

Hour Number	Percent In Seat	Recorder
5	12	Rambo
6	57	Littlejohn

a. The baseline record reveals that Pat's percentage of in-seat behavior ranged from _____ to _____% per session and averaged _____%.

b. Was the baseline conducted long enough to ensure that no drastic changes in the operant level occurred?

c. Was the final baseline session percentage as low or lower than the previous session?

d. Are more baseline data required? Why or why not?

Answers are found on pages 204 and 205.

SUMMARY

The operant level describes the occurrence of the behavior before instruction begins. It is determined by taking a baseline, which is the period of time during which a behavior is observed and measured prior to the instructional intervention. Determining the operant level during a baseline condition permits the objective measurement of the occurrence of a behavior and helps in evaluating a program's effectiveness.

Two methods of taking baseline measurements are by frequency counting, which consists of tallying the number of times the behavior occurs during a specified period of time, and by time sampling, which consists of recording whether or not the behavior occurred during a specified period.

To determine whether or not an adequate baseline has been established so that instruction can begin, you should consider the following questions: (1) Does the baseline adequately show the range (variability) of the behavior? and (2) Is the final baseline data point as low or lower than the data point from the previous baseline session or day? When sufficient baseline data have been collected so that both questions can be answered yes, the intervention can begin.

SUGGESTED READINGS

Craighead, W. E., Kazdin, A. E., & Mahoney, M. J. *Behavior modification: Principles, issues, and applications.* Boston: Houghton-Mifflin, 1976.

Gambrill, E. D. (Ed.). *Behavior modification: Handbook of assessment, intervention and evaluation.* San Francisco: Jossey-Bass, 1977.

Thompson, T. I., & Grabowski, J. (Eds.). *Behavior modification of the mentally retarded.* New York: Oxford University Press, 1972.

Review Set 11

1. The o_____ l_____ describes the occurrence of the behavior before instruction or intervention begins.

2. A b_____ is the period of time during which a behavior is observed and measured before instruction begins.

3. Determining the operant level via a baseline allows the o_____ measurement of a behavior's occurrence and helps in evaluating the effectiveness of the program.

4. One method of determining an operant level is to t_____ the number of times the behavior occurs. This method is called f_____ c_____.

5. Another method of determining an operant level is t_____ s_____, in which you record whether or not the behavior occurred during a specified period.

6. The two questions you must ask to determine whether you have collected sufficient baseline data are: (a) Does the baseline adequately show the r_____ (variability) of the behavior? and (b) Is the final baseline d_____ p_____ as low or lower than the previous data point?

The answers are on page 205.

CHAPTER 12

Program Measurement
and Evaluation

This chapter will tell you how to measure and evaluate your program's success. We'll consider several issues: measuring the reliability of the behavioral recording, using two methods to record the behaviors during the instructional intervention, and determining by graphs and criterion levels whether a program is working.

In the previous chapter we briefly discussed the critical role of observing behaviors. You learned that to determine the student's operant level, or behavior prior to the intervention, it was necessary to record the behavior during a baseline period. As you now know, the baseline (1) allows the objective measurement of the occurrence of a behavior, and (2) helps you determine the effectiveness of a program after the intervention begins by comparing the baseline level of behavior to the level after the intervention. If the behavior has increased substantially during the intervention, the program has been effective. The best way to determine the effectiveness of a program is to set a criterion level for success before beginning instruction.

Let's reconsider frequency counting and time sampling, this time to see how these two recording methods can be used during an intervention to objectively determine when a program is not working. (Note: There are a number of ways of recording behaviors besides the two already discussed. For more information, consult the lists of suggested readings at the end of this and the previous chapter.)

FREQUENCY COUNTING

Frequency counting was introduced in the previous chapter as a procedure in which you count the number of times a specific

151

behavior occurs within a set period of time. For example, Ms. McDonald has been working with Ann, a student in her class who needs to have her self-feeding responses increased. Before beginning a program to increase Ann's independent use of a spoon at meals, Ms. McDonald must conduct a baseline to determine how often it occurs. Since Ann's self-feeding behavior is discrete and countable, Ms. McDonald decides to use the frequency counting method. Specifically, she's interested in knowing the number of times Ann will independently feed herself with a spoon at the lunch meal.

Obtaining Reliable Records

One concern that Ms. McDonald had was that there would be times at lunch when she would be occupied with another student and her aide, Ms. Valentine, would be responsible for recording whether or not Ann had used her spoon. Ms. McDonald wasn't concerned about whether or not Ms. Valentine would do the recording but rather whether or not she and Ms. Valentine would observe and record self-feeding in the same way. The problem was that Ann would sometimes raise the spoonful of food to her mouth but not eat it. She would instead hold the spoon in her mouth for a few moments and then return it to the plate. After that she would raise the spoon to her mouth and actually eat the food. Thus, it was sometimes difficult to determine if she had actually taken a bite.

Before recording could begin, then, Ms. McDonald knew that she and Ms. Valentine would need to develop some criterion by which a bite would be counted. They discussed the problem and decided to count only those times that Ann placed the spoonful of food in her mouth and removed an empty spoon. The criterion was worded as a behavioral objective (see Chapter 1). In this way Ms. McDonald could feel more confident that both of them would record the same behavior; however, she still couldn't prove that, in fact, they would both agree on each observed response.

In behavioral terms, Ms. McDonald's problem concerned whether or not there would be *interobserver reliability* or agreement regarding Ann's self-feeding.

> Interobserver reliability is a measure of the degree to which two or more observers agree that a specific behavior occurred.

Interobserver reliability is an important concern because it's extremely rare that a single individual records and conducts a student's program. As a result, it's important that everyone responsible for recording or conducting the program agree that the behavior occurred. Otherwise instances of the behavior may be missed by some individuals and not be recorded or reinforced when in fact the behavior did occur. Lack of interobserver reliability is especially crucial when the behavior is first being established through a continuous reinforcement schedule or is being shaped. In both cases, it is extremely important that all appropriate instances of the behavior be reinforced.

Calculating Reliability

In calculating reliability we're interested in determining whether two or more persons who are observing a student agree that a specific behavior occurred. Continuing with our example, Ms. McDonald decided to determine interobserver reliability between herself and Ms. Valentine. To do so, they both observed Ann during lunch and independently recorded her self-feeding. In order to synchronize their records, they divided the recording sheet into 30-second intervals of time. At the end of the lunch their records were as shown.

Recorder: McDonald	Type of Recording: Frequency	Recorder: Valentine	Type of Recording: Frequency
Student: Ann	Date:	Student: Ann	Date:
Behavior: Self-feeding with a spoon	September 6	Behavior: Self-feeding with a spoon	September 6
Condition: Baseline		Condition: Baseline	

Interval	Behavior Occurred	Interval	Behavior Occurred
1		1	
2		2	
3	/	3	/
4		4	
5		5	
6		6	
7	/	7	/
8		8	
9	/	9	/
10		10	
11	/	11	/
12		12	
13		13	
14		14	

Interval	Behavior Occurred	Interval	Behavior Occurred
15	/	15	/
16		16	
17		17	
18		18	
19	/	19	/
20	/	20	
21	/	21	/
22		22	
23		23	
24		24	
25		25	
26		26	
27		27	
28		28	
29		29	
30		30	
Total	8	Total	7

One way of calculating the interobserver reliability or the percentage of agreement between the observers is to use the following formula:

$$\text{interobserver reliability} = \frac{\text{number of times observers agreed}}{\text{number of times observers agreed} + \text{number of times observers disagreed}} \times 100 = \text{percentage of agreement}$$

Using this formula we can calculate the agreement (interobserver reliability) between Ms. McDonald and Ms. Valentine on the number of times Ann fed herself with a spoon on September 6. First we must determine the number of times they agreed and disagreed. Looking at their recording sheets we see that they agreed that Ann self-fed in Intervals 3, 7, 9, 11, 15, 19, and 21, and disagreed in Interval 20 in that Ms. McDonald saw Ann feed herself, whereas Ms. Valentine did not. Thus, the two agreed in seven instances and disagreed on one. We calculate that their percentage of agreement or reliability score is 87.5%.

$$\text{interobserver reliability} = \frac{7}{7 + 1} \times 100 = 87.5\%$$

A second way to determine reliability when frequency data are recorded is to divide the lower number by the higher number and multiply the result by 100. In this case, Ms. Valentine had the lower number of recorded occurrences, seven, while Ms.

McDonald had the higher number, eight. Dividing 7 by 8 and multiplying by 100, we find that their reliability score is again 87.5%. (There are a number of ways to calculate interobserver reliability and some of these methods are quite sophisticated. Interested readers can find a more comprehensive treatment of the topic in some of the publications listed in the suggested readings at the end of the chapter.)

In general, the minimum percentage of interobserver reliability you should accept is above 70% and preferably above 80%. In this case, the two instructors can feel fairly confident that they are both in agreement as to when Ann feeds herself because they agreed on 87.5% of the instances that occurred.

Recording and Evaluating the Baseline and Intervention

Having obtained a satisfactory percentage of interobserver reliability, the instructors continued the baseline recording of Ann's self-feeding. The following chart summarizes Ann's 5-day baseline record.

Student: Ann		Type of Recording: Frequency
Behavior: Self-feeding with a spoon		
Condition: Baseline		
Date	Number of Times Behavior Occurred	Recorder
September 6	8	McDonald
September 7	7	McDonald
September 8	9	Valentine
September 9	6	McDonald
September 10	5	Valentine

The baseline revealed that Ann's self-feeding averaged seven times per lunch and ranged from five to nine times. Ms. McDonald decided to discontinue the baseline condition and begin the intervention program because the baseline was stable and the last data point was lower than the one for the previous lunch (see Chapter 11). She would conduct another interobserver reliability check during the intervention program. To evaluate the success of the intervention program, Ms. McDonald set the following criterion level: after 2 weeks the intervention will increase Ann's self-feeding by 80% over her baseline average.

The intervention condition consisted of reinforcing each self-feeding response with praise, with either Ms. McDonald or Ms.

Valentine saying "Good eating, Ann." The frequency data collected for the first 2 weeks of the social reinforcement of self-feeding follow.

Student: Ann		Type of Recording: Frequency
Behavior: Self-feeding with a spoon		
Condition: Social reinforcement, i.e., praise for self-feeding		

Date	Number of Times Behavior Occurred	Recorder
September 13	12	McDonald
September 14	15	Valentine
September 15	16	Valentine
September 16	18	McDonald
September 17	14	Valentine
September 20	18	Valentine
September 21	19	McDonald
September 22	16	McDonald
September 23	23	Valentine
September 24	25	Valentine

Ms. McDonald decided to graph Ann's baseline and treatment records because it would offer her a visual representation of how well the social reinforcement program was working.

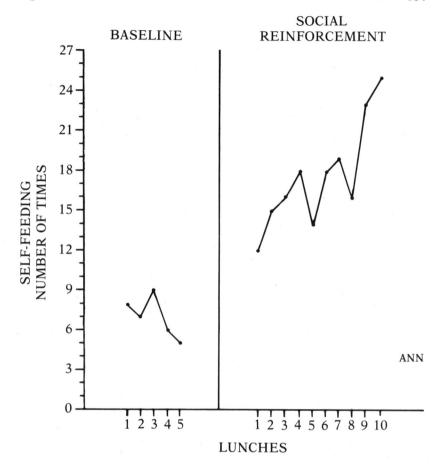

After comparing the records (Ann's frequency of self-feeding) before and after social reinforcement was instituted, Ms. McDonald was pleased to find that the social reinforcement was indeed increasing Ann's self-feeding beyond the 80% criterion level for success. During the social reinforcement condition, Ann's self-feeding averaged 17.6 times per lunch, which represented a 151% increase over the baseline average $(17.6-7=10.6\div7=151\%)$, whereas the criterion level had only been 80%. As a result, Ms. McDonald continued the social reinforcement until Ann would eat her entire meal.

You can see how much easier it is to determine whether a procedure is working when you look at a graph versus a recording sheet. Even before the percentage increase was calculated, the graph very quickly and clearly showed that Ann's self-feeding

behavior increased steadily during the social reinforcement program. It's a good idea to graph the baseline and treatment records
for each behavior you seek to increase. Doing so will enable you
to make better decisions concerning the effectiveness of your
treatment or instructional program. Also, a graph is easily and
quickly understood by parents, administrators, and other staff.

Let's look at another example of frequency counting. Ms.
McDonald wanted to increase Betty's walking behavior. Betty
had some physical defects that made it difficult to walk, but she
could walk; the problem was that Betty didn't like to walk. This
had created another problem because her legs had weakened
from lack of use. Ms. McDonald designated Betty's target
behavior as walking 5 feet when she is given the instruction
"Walk to me." Training sessions were to be 5 minutes in length
and the instruction would be given every 15 seconds.

After six sessions of baseline recording, Ms. McDonald began
a reinforcement program in which Betty was reinforced with an
edible and praise each time she followed the instruction and
walked the 5 feet to Ms. McDonald. The criterion level of success
was a 100% increase over baseline in walking after 5 days of the
reinforcement program. The baseline data indicated that Betty
walked an average of one time per session.

Here is a graph that shows Betty's walking during the baseline and through five sessions of the edible and social reinforcement program.

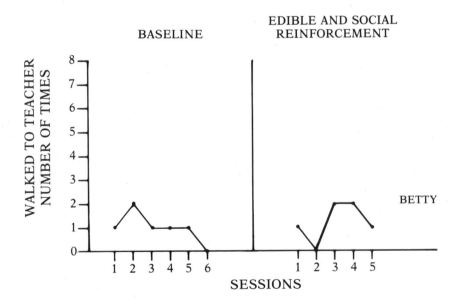

The graph shows that the edible and social reinforcement had very little, if any, effect on Betty's walking, since there was little difference between her frequency of walking before or during training. Her baseline average of walking was 1 time per session and her average during the edible and social reinforcement program was 1.2 times per session, or a 20% increase over baseline. Thus, the criterion level for success was not achieved. As a result, Ms. McDonald decided to stop the edible and social reinforcement program and try a vibratory reinforcement program. In the vibratory reinforcement program, Betty received 5 seconds of vibratory stimulation from a vibrator placed on her arm. Social reinforcement, that is, praise, was still given. After Ms. McDonald had conducted the vibratory reinforcement program for five sessions, the graph looked as shown.

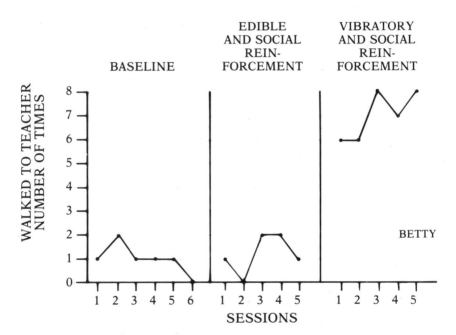

The graph shows clearly that the vibratory reinforcement produced a rapid increase in Betty's walking. During the five sessions that the vibratory program was in effect, Betty's walking averaged seven times per session. Thus, the vibratory reinforcement increased Betty's walking by 700% relative to the baseline. (The baseline average was 1 time per session, vibratory reinforcement average was 7 times per session, 7/1 x 100 = 700% increase from baseline.) This easily surpassed the criterion level for success of 100%. As a result, Ms. McDonald continued to use the vibratory reinforcement program and gradually lengthened the distance that Betty had to walk in order to be reinforced.

Again, you can see how helpful it is to graph your program data or records. When records are graphed, it's immediately apparent whether or not a training program is working. If your graph shows that it isn't, add another reinforcer(s) to the existing program, look for other problems and then try again, or discontinue the existing program and try another.

Practice Set 12A

Betty also needed to learn to follow other simple instructions such as "Sit down" and "Stand up." Here are the training programs that Ms. McDonald instituted to increase Betty's sitting down and standing up. The vibratory and social reinforcement program was used with both behaviors because it had been used effectively to increase Betty's walking behavior. For both behaviors, the criterion level for success for the reinforcement program was a 300% increase over the baseline average after 10 training sessions.

After 10 sessions of training, the graph for training sitting down looked like this.

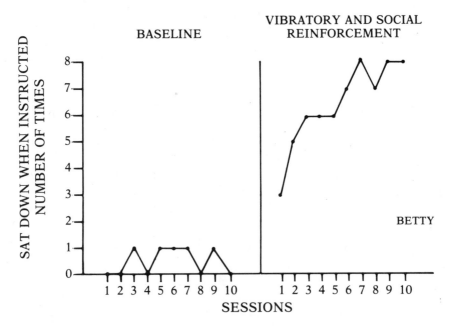

Answer the following questions.

1. Was the baseline assessment adequate? Why?

2. Was the reinforcement program effective?

3. What was the baseline average for sitting down? The training average?

4. By what percent was sitting down increased in the training phase?

5. Was the criterion level for success achieved?

After 10 sessions of training, Betty's graph for standing up looked like this.

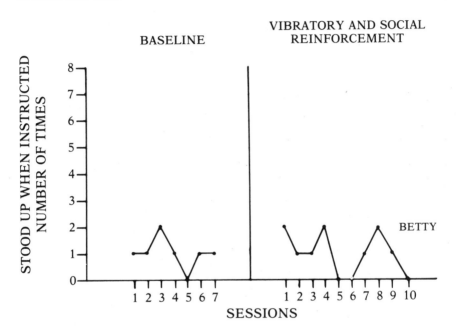

Answer the following questions.

6. Was the baseline assessment adequate?

7. What was the baseline average of standing up? The training average?

8. Was the reinforcement program effective?

9. What should Ms. McDonald do?

Answers are found on page 205.

TIME SAMPLING

Time sampling was introduced in the previous chapter as a procedure in which you observe the student at fixed intervals for a specified period of time and then record whether or not the behavior occurred. The behavior can then be expressed as a percentage of the total number of observation intervals.

Ms. Marks would like to increase John's on-task behavior during a 10-minute finger painting task. Ms. Marks will determine interobserver reliability once during the baseline and once during the reinforcement condition.

During the baseline, John will be observed every minute for 5 seconds. Thus, there will be a total of 10 observations each time. Interobserver reliability between Ms. Marks and her aide, Mr. Armstrong, will be conducted during the first baseline observation session. At the end of the session their records look as follows.

Recorder: Marks	Recorder: Armstrong
Student: John	Student: John
Behavior: On Task	Behavior: On Task
Condition: Baseline	Condition: Baseline
Type of Recording: Time sampling	Type of Recording: Time sampling
Date: January 20	Date: January 20

Minutes

1	2	3	4	5
✔			✔	
6	7	8	9	10
✔		✔		

Minutes

1	2	3	4	5
✔			✔	
6	7	8	9	10
✔		✔		✔

Total Observation Intervals 10

Total Observation Intervals
   in Which Behavior Occurred 4

Percentage of Time On Task 40%

Total Observation Intervals 10

Total Observation Intervals
   in Which Behavior Occurred 5

Percentage of Time On Task 50%

As noted before, to calculate interobserver reliability we must first determine the number of times the observers agreed and disagreed. Inspecting the baseline record, we find that they agreed in every observation interval except the 10th. We'll exclude those observation intervals in which neither observer reported seeing the behavior occur, in this case, Intervals 2, 3, 5, 7, and 9. Thus, the two observers agreed on four instances and disagreed on one. Using the interobserver reliability formula we can calculate their percentage of agreement or reliability score:

$$\text{interobserver reliability} = \frac{4}{4 + 1} \times 100 = 80\%$$

Having obtained a satisfactory interobserver reliability score, Ms. Marks continued the baseline recordings of John's on-task behavior. A summary of the baseline record follows. The baseline sessions were conducted on January 20 and 21.

Student: John   Type of Recording: Time sampling
Behavior: On Task
Condition: Baseline

	Number of Intervals (1 min.) in Which Behavior Was Observed	Total Number of Observation Intervals	Percentage of Time Behavior Occurred	Recorder
Date: January 20				
Session 1	4	10	40	Marks
Session 2	3	10	30	Armstrong
Date: January 21				
Session 3	5	10	50	Armstrong
Session 4	4	10	40	Marks

Average Percentage of Time 40%

The brief four-session baseline (four 10-minute observation sessions) showed that John was on task in an average of 40% of the intervals. Because the baseline had been conducted for a sufficient period, Ms. Marks began the reinforcement condition. In the reinforcement condition, John was reinforced every 45 seconds with a small piece of candy and the praise "Good working, John." Ms. Marks' criterion for deciding whether the reinforcement procedure was effectively increasing John's on-task behavior was if there was a 100% increase over baseline within five sessions. Each session would still be 10 minutes in length.

The intervention records for the first five sessions of the reinforcement procedure are shown here.

Student: John   Type of Recording: Time sampling
Behavior: On Task
Condition: Reinforcement
  FI 45 seconds

	Number of Intervals (1 min.) in Which Behavior Was Observed	Total Number of Observation Intervals	Percentage of Time Behavior Occurred	Recorder
Date: January 22				
Session 1	4	10	40	Marks
Session 2	5	10	50	Armstrong

	Number of Intervals (1 min.) in Which Behavior Was Observed	Total Number of Observation Intervals	Percentage of Time Behavior Occurred	Recorder
Date: January 23				
Session 3	5	10	50	Marks
Session 4	6	10	60	Marks
Date: January 24				
Session 5	5	10	50	Armstrong
Average Percentage of Time 50%				

The graph displaying the intervention records for the five sessions of the 45-second FI reinforcement procedure follows.

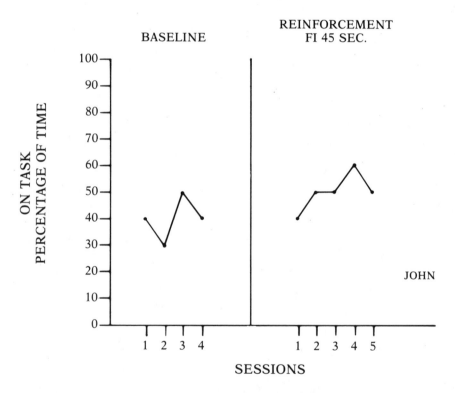

The graph shows that John's on-task behavior during the finger painting activity averaged 50% during the five sessions that the FI 45-second reinforcement procedure was in effect. Since the reinforcement procedure had not increased John's on-task behavior by 100% of baseline (80% of time on task), the chosen criterion, Ms. Marks shortened the FI interval to 15 seconds. By doing so, she hoped to increase John's on-task behavior by providing more frequent reinforcement for the behavior.

The records for the first five sessions of the 15-second FI reinforcement procedure are shown here.

Student: John   Type of Recording: Time sampling
Behavior: On Task
Condition: Reinforcement
  FI 15 seconds

	Number of Intervals (1 min.) in Which Behavior Was Observed	Total Number of Observation Intervals	Percentage of Time Behavior Occurred	Recorder
Date: January 27				
Session 1	7	10	70	Armstrong
Session 2	8	10	80	Marks
Date: January 28				
Session 3	9	10	90	Armstrong
Session 4	8	10	80	Armstrong
Date: January 29				
Session 5	10	10	100	Marks

Average Percentage of Time 84%

In Session 4, interobserver reliability was assessed. Both observers, Marks and Armstrong, observed John to be on task in the same eight intervals, thereby yielding a perfect 100% reliability score.

After five 10-minute sessions of the FI 15-second reinforcement program, John's graph looked as shown on the following page.

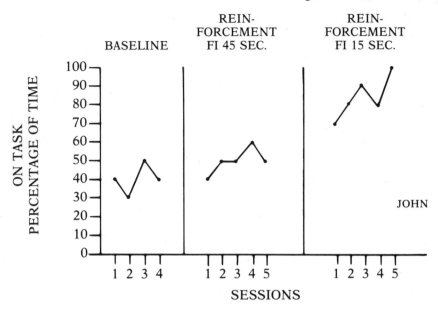

The graph shows clearly that the FI 15-second reinforcement procedure produced a rapid increase in John's on-task behavior. During the five sessions of the FI 15-second reinforcement procedure, John's on-task behavior averaged 84% versus 40 and 50% in the respective baseline and FI 45-second reinforcement conditions. The FI 15-second reinforcement program had raised John's on-task behavior above the 100% above baseline criterion level of success (or 80% on task) that Ms. Marks had set. Thus, she lengthened the interval of time between reinforcers to 30 seconds (FI 30 seconds). Ultimately she planned to reinforce John's on-task behavior every 2 minutes (FI 2 minutes). (Note: Ms. Marks' mistake had been setting too long an FI interval, 45 seconds, in the beginning of the reinforcement program.)

Practice Set 12B

    After inspecting each graph, answer the questions.

1.

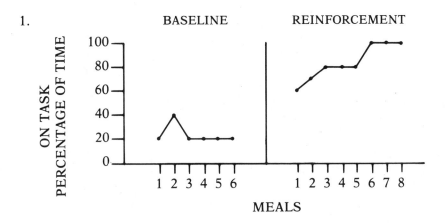

    a. Was the baseline assessment adequate?

    b. Was the reinforcement procedure effective?

2.

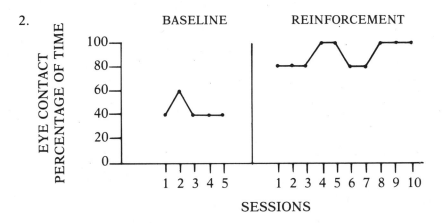

    a. What was the baseline average for eye contact?

    b. What was the training average for eye contact?

    Answer the following questions.

3. Two child care workers were attempting to measure inter-observer reliability. Their recording sheets looked as follows.

	Observer 1 Seconds					
	10	20	30	40	50	60
Minute 1	✔		✔		✔	
Minute 2	✔		✔		✔	
Minute 3	✔		✔			✔

	Observer 2 Seconds					
	10	20	30	40	50	60
Minute 1	✔		✔			
Minute 2	✔		✔		✔	
Minute 3	✔					✔

   a. What was their interobserver reliability score?

   b. What percentage of the time did each observer record that the behavior occurred?

4. Ms. Norton is teaching Billy to say "Mm." She has set her criterion level for success as an 80% increase above the baseline average after five sessions. Here is the graph showing the baseline and five sessions of the speech training program.

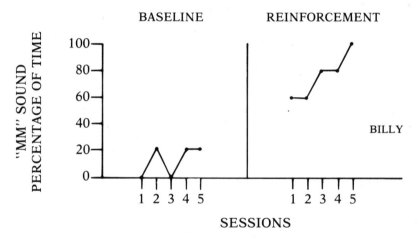

   a. What was the baseline average?

   b. What was the average during the training condition?

   c. During the reinforcement procedure, what was the percentage increase from baseline?

   d. Should Ms. Norton continue the reinforcement procedure she has been using?

The answers are on page 206.

SUMMARY

In order to evaluate the success of a program you must have an adequate baseline, an acceptable level of interobserver reliability in the baseline and treatment conditions, and a criterion level of success by which the training procedure will be judged.

Before recording data, observers need to agree on exactly which behaviors are to be counted or measured. Interobserver reliability is the measure of the degree to which two or more observers agree that a specific behavior occurred. Determining reliability is important for ensuring that records are accurate and occurrences of the behavior are properly reinforced. Interobserver reliability is calculated by either dividing the number of times the observers agreed that the behavior occurred by the number of times they agreed plus disagreed, and multiplying by 100, or dividing the lower number by the higher, and multiplying by 100. These formulas give the percentage of agreement between observers. The minimum acceptable percentage is above 70%, while it is preferable to have it above 80%.

A training procedure to increase a behavior is evaluated by comparing the level of behavior during training to its baseline level. A graph provides a quick and easy visual way of determining the effectiveness of a procedure. You should also set a criterion level of success by which each procedure will be judged. This criterion level is usually a minimum percentage by which the behavior must be increased within a specified number of days or sessions. If the procedure fails to meet the criterion level, then it should be revised or replaced with another procedure.

SUGGESTED READINGS

Bijou, S. W., Peterson, R. F., & Ault, M. H. A method to integrate descriptive and experimental field studies at the level of data and empirical concepts. *Journal of Applied Behavior Analysis*, 1968, *1*, 175-191.

Hersen, M., & Bellack, A. S. *Behavioral assessment: A practical handbook.* Elmsford, N.Y.: Pergamon Press, 1976.

Johnson, S. M., & Bolstad, O. D. Methodological issues in naturalistic observation: Some problems and solutions for field research. In L. A. Hamerlynck, J. Handy, & D. A. Mash (Eds.), *Behavior change: Methodology, concepts, and practice.* Champaign, Ill.: Research Press, 1973.

Kazdin, A. E. Methodological and assessment considerations in evaluating reinforcement programs in applied settings. *Journal of Applied Behavior Analysis*, 1973, *6*, 517-531.

Repp, A. C., Roberts, D. M., Slack, D. J., Repp, C. F., & Berkler, M. S. A comparison of frequency, interval, and time-sampling methods of data collection. *Journal of Applied Behavior Analysis*, 1976, *9*, 501-508.

Review Set 12

1. F_____ counting measures the number of times a student performs a specific behavior within a set period of time.

2. Before recording can begin, observers must decide upon a c_____ by which to measure or record the behavior.

3. I_____ r_____ is a measure of the degree to which two or more observers agree that a specific behavior occurred.

4. One method of calculating interobserver reliability is to divide the number of times the observers a_____ that the behavior occurred by the number of times they a_____ plus the number of times they d_____, and multiply by 100.

5. Another method of calculating interobserver reliability when frequency records are collected is to divide the l_____ number recorded by the h_____ number recorded, and multiply by 100.

6. The minimum interobserver reliability percentage that is acceptable is above _____.

7. A c_____ level of success for an intervention is the specification of a percentage increase above the baseline average that must be achieved within a specified training period.

8. A g_____ offers a visual representation of the effectiveness of a treatment program.

9. In t_____ s_____ recording the student is observed at fixed intervals for a specified period of time to determine whether or not a specific behavior occurred during each observation interval.

Answers are found on page 206.

CHAPTER 13

The Development of Lasting Programs: Generalization, Behavior Maintenance, Program Pitfalls, and Guidelines for Establishing Behavioral Programs

You learned how to measure and evaluate the results of your behavioral programs in the last two chapters. Now, in this chapter, we'll consider four other important concerns regarding behavioral or educational programs: generalization training, the maintenance of behavior change, potential programming pitfalls, and guidelines for establishing successful programs. Generalization training and the maintenance of behavior change will be discussed first because scientific evidence indicates that the student's newly learned skills or behaviors don't automatically transfer to new settings and situations or necessarily continue to occur after the termination of the behavioral program. Thus, because your students' performance is likely to be situation specific, you should learn how to program for generalization and the maintenance of the educational or therapeutic effect. We'll then consider some of the pitfalls you must avoid in order to ensure that your behavioral programs are successful and conclude with a discussion of some useful guidelines you may follow for creating behavioral programs that are humane, ethical, beneficial, enduring, and successful.

GENERALIZATION TRAINING

> Generalization training is a procedure for transferring control over behavior in one situation to other situations.

We want our students to display their newly learned skills in a variety of situations or environments. When they do, we say that their behavior has generalized or that generalization has taken place. Unfortunately, students rarely spontaneously display learning or therapy gains in a new setting or situation. Thus, skills learned in the classroom don't automatically transfer to the home or the residential facility, skills learned in a one-to-one session don't automatically transfer to group sessions, and skills learned from one instructor don't automatically transfer to another instructor. A major reason generalization rarely occurs is that most students, even the most severely intellectually impaired, can *discriminate* between situations and settings such as home and the classroom, one-to-one sessions and group sessions, and different instructors. As a result, if we want generalization to occur, we must program for it. The means by which we do this is called generalization training.

Generalization training can be accomplished either during or after a behavioral program. Thus, you can implement generalization training while the student is in the process of learning a new behavior or after the behavior has been learned. There are several ways of facilitating generalization.

Emphasize common elements between new settings and the original training setting. You can help your students learn to generalize by ensuring that the discriminative stimuli and reinforcing consequences from the original setting are present in the new settings. For instance, if you want a student to give eye contact to her mother or another instructor, make sure that they use the same verbal prompt and edible reinforcer that you used to obtain eye contact.

Use an intermittent reinforcement schedule in the original training situation. Using an intermittent reinforcement schedule helps to ensure that the desired behavior is maintained (response or behavior maintenance will be described shortly) and facilitates generalization in any new settings. Scientific research has shown that intermittently reinforced behaviors are more likely to generalize than continuously reinforced behaviors.

Teach the student the behavior under a variety of conditions. The more conditions in which the student performs the behavior, the more likely it is that her behavior will generalize to new situations. For example, if you want to increase the likelihood that the student will eat with a spoon at home, have several different instructors teach her to eat with a spoon in several different situations at school, such as while the student is alone, sitting at a table with others, or in different rooms. Research has indicated that generalization is more likely to occur when several different instructors train the student in several different situations or settings.

Add auxiliary discriminative stimuli to the new situation. After you've been successfully using behavioral programs with your students, there may be some discriminative stimuli that exercise a great deal of control over several of the students' other behaviors. For instance, the verbal prompt "Do this" or a gestural prompt such as pointing to an object may have been used to teach several different behaviors in the past. By adding these discriminative stimuli to the original training session and the new training situations, you'll be increasing the prospects for generalization to occur. Or you can simply add them to the new situations or settings. Keep in mind, however, that these supplemental discriminative stimuli must be faded once a student's behavior has generalized.

Change from artificial reinforcers to natural ones in the original training situation. By doing this, you can greatly facilitate the generalization process, as well as response or behavior maintenance. For example, you should try to eliminate reliance on edibles whenever possible and switch instead to social reinforcers such as praise, since it's much more likely that the student will receive some form of praise for her successful efforts in a variety of situations than that she will receive edibles.

BEHAVIOR OR RESPONSE MAINTENANCE

No matter how spectacularly a behavioral procedure has increased an appropriate behavior, such success is meaningless if the appropriate behavior disappears once the procedure is discontinued. To ensure that this doesn't happen, we must be concerned about maintaining the effect of our intervention. We can never assume that the effect will be maintained after the program is withdrawn; consequently, we must program for the maintenance of the behavior or effect.

There are several procedures that can be used to increase the likelihood that the newly learned behavior will be maintained. Note that there's not much difference between these procedures and the procedures that facilitate generalization training. (In fact, some of the same procedures are used in both cases.) This is because behavior maintenance is an integral part of generalization training.

Substitute naturally occurring reinforcers for the artificial or programmed reinforcers that were used to increase the behavior initially. Although artificial reinforcers are often necessary to effectively increase the behavior, they should be phased out once the behavior is occurring at the desired level and more natural reinforcers should be substituted. Furthermore, the use of artificial reinforcers together with the natural reinforcer may, in fact, enhance the subsequent effectiveness of the natural reinforcer. For example, the simultaneous use of an edible and praise during eye contact training sessions increases the likelihood that the praise (or attention) alone will maintain eye contact after the student has learned to give eye contact. Or praise can be used to reinforce proper eating with a spoon and then be gradually eliminated as the student begins eating with a spoon. At that point the natural reinforcer (a bite of food) that follows the correct eating response (use of a spoon) should be sufficient to maintain proper eating.

Train other individuals in the student's life, such as relatives or residential caretakers, to carry out your behavioral program. To ensure that the student's newly learned behaviors will be maintained at home, on another shift, over the summer, or in his new classroom during the coming school year, you should train "significant others" to carry out your successful behavioral program in other settings. This point can't be stressed enough, since research has shown, for example, that autistic children whose parents didn't learn behavioral techniques or who were institutionalized in facilities where the staff members were untrained in the techniques regressed and lost the skills they had been taught.

Gradually remove or fade the behavioral consequences. The student should become less and less dependent on the consequences. The less dependent a student is on structured behavioral consequences or reinforcers, the more he will be prepared for normalization, that is, functioning under the same types of contingencies and consequences as normal persons. This is important because the real world provides much less structure and fewer immediate behavioral consequences, especially reinforcing ones. In the case of severely and profoundly retarded students, you probably wouldn't be fading or gradually removing the behavioral consequences for some time, since this technique works best when the student is capable of performing a variety of complex behaviors. For instance, you could fade or attenuate the reinforcing consequences for a student who is being phased into a "more normal" classroom. It would be important for this student to learn to perform a variety of complex behaviors in a variety of situations for varying lengths of time in order for him to function successfully in his new environment. By gradually fading the structured behavioral consequences given in the student's old classroom environment, you would be preparing him for his new "lifestyle." Of course, you'd never fade all reinforcing consequences because, if you did, the student's behavior would extinguish.

Vary the training conditions. This will keep the student from discriminating when a consequence or reinforcer is likely to occur. The best way to prevent the student from discriminating by picking up cues regarding when and where the consequences will be delivered and by whom is to train the behavior in a variety of settings with several individuals delivering the consequences. This, of course, constitutes generalization training.

Use intermittent schedules of reinforcement. Intermittent schedules make the student's behavior more resistant to extinction. As mentioned previously in the discussion on generalization training, intermittent reinforcement schedules are ideal for maintaining a desirable behavior. You should make every effort to ensure that the schedule of reinforcement becomes more and more intermittent. (The technical term that describes this process is *attenuation* or attenuating the reinforcement schedule.) This, of course, also prepares the student for a more "normal" way of life because many of the reinforcers that individuals normally receive are on an extremely intermittent schedule, such as being complimented by your supervisor.

Increasingly delay the delivery of reinforcers. In this way the student will learn not to expect immediate reinforcement following his performance of an appropriate behavior. Although it's crucial that behavior be established by immediate reinforcement, it's unrealistic and unwieldy to continue to immediately reinforce the student each time the behavior occurs. Furthermore, immediate reinforcement is counter to the spirit of normalization, since most of our reinforcers, especially social and monetary ones, are delivered only after a lot of time has passed. A good example of the importance of building in reinforcement delays is moving a student from a one-to-one training situation to a group instructional setting where several students may be seated around a table. If the student is to succeed in such a situation, he must have learned to accept a delay in the delivery of his reinforcers. Accordingly, you would begin delaying the delivery of reinforcers while he was still in the one-to-one training setting and only transfer him to a group instructional setting when he could tolerate the same reinforcement delays that exist in the group setting.

PROGRAMMING PITFALLS

There are several pitfalls that you should avoid as you establish and carry out your behavioral programs. You can avoid these pitfalls by following these suggestions.

Don't attempt to increase complex behaviors until you become thoroughly proficient as a behavior change agent. Rather, work on increasing simple behaviors until you've achieved a sufficient amount of expertise.

Don't expect too much too soon from the student. Even though behavioral techniques are highly effective in increasing behavior, the speed with which they will work depends on a multitude of factors, such as your expertise, the characteristics of the student, and the learning environment. There are no hard and fast rules on how rapidly a behavior should increase. Therefore, the best way to ensure that you are maximizing the learning process is to evaluate, on a regular basis, all the factors in your program and in the learning environment.

Don't change a program or discontinue it until you've thoroughly analyzed why it may not be working. Ask yourself these questions:

1. Does the student know what is expected of her? You can answer this question for nonverbal students by making sure that your behavioral objectives are reasonable, clear cut, and have appropriate criterion levels. For verbal students, simply tell or show them what you expect.

2. Do all of the change agents in the environment (all instructors, parents, and volunteers) understand the program? You should always make sure that everyone is very familiar with the program. Never set up a program without informing everyone of what you are doing and gaining their cooperation with the program.

3. Are all of the change agents motivated to participate in the program and help ensure that it works? Often change agents aren't motivated to participate or to agree to participate in a program when they don't feel adequately informed or involved. By involving them early in the design of the program, you may avoid the problems of apathy and sabotage and may gain their willingness to make the necessary sacrifices to ensure the success of your program.

4. Are the reinforcers working as they should? If it appears that the student isn't under the control of the reinforcers being used, you should evaluate and possibly change the following variables: the type of reinforcer (is it really a reinforcer?), the schedule of reinforcement, the amount of reinforcer being given, and the immediacy with which the reinforcer is delivered.

5. Is the program being applied consistently and correctly? Failure to consistently apply the program is probably the

most common reason why reinforcement programs fail to increase behavior.

GUIDELINES FOR ESTABLISHING PROGRAMS

You've now learned the behavioral and educational principles in this book and are ready to apply them; but before you do, you should carefully consider the following suggestions and guidelines. Once you have, you will be ready to begin effectively increasing the behavior of your students.

Know thyself. Don't consider changing the behavior of others until you've gained some insight into your own behavior. Understanding why you behave as you do will help you become a proficient and humane behavior modifier.

Know the student. You should always strive to learn as much about your students as possible. The only way to do so is to work directly with them. This point can't be overstressed, especially in regard to professionals who are responsible for designing programs but who spend little time with the individuals for whom those programs are intended. Knowing your students' strengths and weaknesses will ensure that they are developmentally ready to benefit from whatever programs you have selected for them.

Know that the program will be beneficial for the student. No program should be used simply because it will keep the student busy, because certain educational materials must be used, or because it makes the student less annoying or inconvenient to work with. Rather, a program should only be used if it will further the student's progress toward a normal, productive, happy, or worthwhile life.

Develop a value system that respects the dignity of the student and that operates on the principle of fairness. Our students deserve fairness and respect, as does everyone. You will be demonstrating that you're fair and respect the student if you (1) don't apply procedures arbitrarily, (2) don't refuse to use a procedure simply because of personal bias, such as refusing to use edible reinforcers simply because you don't believe in using them, (3) always attempt to use a systematic approach in modifying the student's behavior and evaluate that approach, (4) don't refuse to seek help from other instructors, aides, or consultants because you think that such assistance would make you appear incompetent, and (5) systematically evaluate your own performance from time to time to ensure that you are correctly carrying out the various procedures you're using with your students.

Keep everyone informed about your programs. If your program is well designed and based on sound behavioral and educational principles, then you should have no qualms about informing a student's parents and the facility administration about what you're doing. By keeping all concerned parties informed about all your various programs, you'll be demonstrating your competence and concern for your students.

Any system can be misused and abused by the individuals who are responsible for designing and implementing it. Knowledge is power and people with power must take the responsibility to use that power in beneficial ways. Behavioral techniques are powerful procedures that can be useful or damaging depending on how they are used. You now have the power to increase behavior with behavioral techniques and the responsibility to use that power wisely.

SUMMARY

For behavioral programs to be considered successful, students must display their newly learned behaviors or skills in a variety of situations and settings long after the termination of the initial training programs. Unfortunately, this doesn't happen automatically, so generalization and maintenance of behaviors must be programmed. Generalization training is the way that control over behavior in one situation is transferred to other situations. Several ways of facilitating generalization are emphasizing common elements between new settings and the original training setting; using an intermittent reinforcement schedule in the original training; teaching the behavior under various conditions; using prompts; and shifting from artificial reinforcers to natural ones in the original training situation.

Behavior maintenance is an integral part of generalization training, so the procedures for both are very similar. Some maintenance procedures are substituting natural reinforcers for artificial ones; training other individuals in the student's life to carry out your program; fading behavioral consequences; varying the training conditions; using intermittent schedules of reinforcement; and increasingly delaying the delivery of reinforcers.

Three major pitfalls should be avoided in carrying out behavioral programs: (1) attempting to increase complex behaviors before having developed sufficient proficiency as a behavior change agent, (2) expecting too much too soon from the student, and (3) changing or discontinuing a program that isn't working without first analyzing why it failed.

Finally, there are several suggested guidelines for establishing effective and humane programs. They include (1) understanding your own behavior as a prerequisite to understanding your students' behavior, (2) learning as much as possible about each student by working directly with her, (3) only choosing those programs that further the student's progress toward a normal, productive life, (4) developing a value system that respects the student's dignity and is fair, and (5) keeping all interested parties informed about your programs.

SUGGESTED READINGS

Birnbrauer, J. S. Some guides to designing behavioral programs. In D. Marholin II (Ed.), *Child behavior therapy.* New York: Gardner Press, 1978.

Birnbrauer, J. S. Mental retardation. In H. Leitenberg (Ed.), *Handbook of behavior modification.* New York: Appleton-Century-Crofts, 1976.

Bricker, W. A., Morgan, D. G., & Grabowski, J. G. Development of maintenance of a behavior modification repertoire of cottage attendants through T.V. feedback. *American Journal of Mental Deficiency,* 1972, 77, 128-136.

Buell, J., Stoddard, P., Harris, F., & Baer, D. M. Collateral social development accompanying reinforcement of outdoor play in a preschool child. *Journal of Applied Behavior Analysis,* 1968, *1,* 167-173.

Stokes, T. F., & Baer, D. M. An implicit technology of generalization. *Journal of Applied Behavior Analysis,* 1977, *10,* 349-367.

Stokes, T. F., Baer, D. M., & Jackson, R. L. Programming the generalization of a greeting response in four retarded children. *Journal of Applied Behavior Analysis,* 1974, 7, 599-610.

Review Set 13

1. G_____ t_____ is a procedure designed to transfer the control over behavior in one situation to other situations.

2. The reason why generalization rarely occurs spontaneously is that students can d_____ between situations.

3. There are several ways of facilitating generalization training: (a) emphasize c_____ elements in the new setting that are shared with the original training setting, (b) use an i_____ r_____ schedule in the original training situation before you institute generalization training, (c) teach the student the behavior under a variety of

c_____, (d) add auxiliary d_____ stimuli to the new situation, and (e) change the r_____ conditions in the original training situation from artificial to natural ones.

4. B_____ m_____ is an integral part of generalization training.

5. There are several procedures that can be used to facilitate behavior maintenance: (a) substitute n_____ occurring reinforcers for artificial ones, (b) t_____ other people in the student's life to carry out your program, (c) gradually remove or f_____ the behavioral consequences, (d) vary the t_____ conditions, (e) use i_____ s_____ of reinforcement, and (f) increasingly d_____ the delivery of reinforcers.

6. There are three pitfalls to avoid when you attempt to establish or carry out a behavioral program: (a) attempting to modify c_____ behaviors before you have become thoroughly proficient as a behavior change agent, (b) expecting too much too soon from the s_____, and (c) changing or discontinuing a program before you have thoroughly a_____ why it is not working.

7. There are several factors to consider when you analyze why a program is not working: (a) Does the student know what is e_____ of her? (b) Do all of the c_____ agents understand the program? (c) Are all of the change agents m_____ to participate in the program? (d) Are the r_____ working as they should? and (e) Is the program being applied c_____ and correctly?

8. The following are guidelines for establishing programs: know t_____, know the s_____, know that the program will be beneficial for the student, develop a behavioral value system that r_____ the dignity of the student and that operates on the principle of f_____, and keep everyone informed about your programs.

9. You will be demonstrating that you are fair and respect the student if you (a) don't apply procedures a_____, (b) don't refuse to use a procedure because of a personal b_____, (c) always attempt to use a s_____ approach in modifying the student's behavior and evaluate that approach, (d) don't refuse to seek h_____ from others, and (e) systematically evaluate your own p_____ periodically.

Answers are found on page 206.

APPENDIX A

Potential Reinforcers

EDIBLES
(Give very small pieces.)

Corn chips
Pretzel pieces
Cookies
Sugared cereals
Candy
Ice cream (spoonful from a cup)
Raisins
Peanuts

Pudding (spoonful from a cup)
Gelatin (spoonful from a cup)
Mini-marshmallows
Potato chips
Fruit (cherries, grapes, orange or apple slices)
Vegetable bits (carrot sticks, celery sticks)
Cheese (cubes, slices)
Popcorn

LIQUIDS
(Give in small sips or a squirt from a squirt bottle.)

Colas, soft drinks
Orange drink, grape drink, cranberry drink
Fruit juices

Milk
Kool-Aid
Water
Decaffeinated coffee
Tea

OBJECTS

Dolls
Mechanical toys
Whistles (too large to be swallowed)
Bracelets
Hats
Rattles
Noisemakers

Colored chips (too large to be swallowed)
Stuffed toy animals
Balloons
Sweatshirts
Ribbons
Key chains
Decals
Balls

ACTIVITIES

Playing catch with the instructor

Playing on the swings

Playing on the jungle gym

Going on the merry-go-round

Running

Playing tag or hide-and-go-seek with the instructor

Going for a walk with the instructor

Playing with a pet

Taking an automobile ride

Swimming

Visiting the instructor's home

Looking through a book or magazine that has colored pictures

Playing in the gym (unstructured play)

Hearing music

Riding on a rocking horse

Finger painting

Playing in a wading pool

Smelling different fragrances

Opening jars with an edible inside

Jumping

Lying on a waterbed

Clapping hands

SOCIAL PRAISE

"Good" or "Good boy or girl."

"Very good."

"I like that."

"That's good."

"I'm glad you did that."

"That's right, ___(name)___."

"You did a good ___(thing)___."

"Good ___(job)___."

"Mmm-hmm."

"Fine."

"You did it. Very good."

"Thank you" or "Thank you very much."

"I'm so happy with you."

"I'm proud of you."

NONVERBAL MESSAGES AND MOVEMENTS

Facial Expressions

Smiling

Showing surprise and delight

Nodding your head in an approving manner

Laughing

Winking

Being Near the Student

Standing near the student

Sitting near the student

Physical Contact

Hugging

Patting

Touching the student's arm

Tickling

Bouncing the student on your knees

Rubbing the student's back
Kissing
Picking the student up
Wrestling
Tousling the student's hair

Playing patty-cake
Holding the student
Holding the student's hand
Touching the student with a
  vibrator

APPENDIX B

Selected Journals

The following list contains journals that regularly publish articles on the use of behavior modification with retarded students.

American Journal of Mental Deficiency. Washington, D.C.: American Association on Mental Deficiency.

Analysis and Intervention in Developmental Disabilities. Elmsford, N.Y.: Pergamon Press, Inc.

Behavior Modification. Beverly Hills, Calif.: Sage Publications.

Behavior Research of Severe Developmental Disabilities. Amsterdam: North-Holland Publishing Co.

Behavior Therapy. New York: Association for Advancement of Behavior Therapy.

Behaviour Research and Therapy. Elmsford, N.Y.: Pergamon Press, Inc.

Child Behavior Therapy. New York: The Haworth Press.

Education and Training of the Mentally Retarded. Reston, Va.: Division on Mental Retardation, The Council for Exceptional Children.

Education and Treatment of Children. Pittsburgh, Pa.: Pressley Ridge School.

Exceptional Children. Reston, Va.: The Council for Exceptional Children.

Journal of Applied Behavior Analysis. Lawrence, Kans.: Society for the Experimental Analysis of Behavior, Inc.

Journal of Autism and Developmental Disorders. New York: Plenum Publishing Corp.

Journal of Behavior Therapy and Experimental Psychiatry. Elmsford, N.Y.: Pergamon Press, Inc.

Journal of Learning Disabilities. Chicago: The Professional Press, Inc.

Journal of School Psychology. New York: The Journal of School Psychology, Inc.

The Journal of Special Education. New York: Grune & Stratton, Inc.

The Journal of the Association for the Severely Handicapped. Seattle: The Association for the Severely Handicapped.

Mental Retardation. Washington, D.C.: American Association on Mental Deficiency.

Teaching Exceptional Children. Reston, Va.: The Council for Exceptional Children.

APPENDIX C

Answers for
Practice and Review Sets

Practice Set 1A

_✓_ 1. *Combs* is a good behavioral verb, not subject to interpretation.

_____ 2. How can anyone be sure that Bobby likes his music therapy class?

_✓_ 3. *Walks* is a good behavioral verb, not subject to interpretation.

_____ 4. How do we know that Mimi knows what are appropriate table manners?

_____ 5. How do we know or determine that Dorothy appreciates attention?

Practice Set 1B

_____ 1. Can John spill the juice? Take 5 minutes to pour? Fill the glass half full?

_✓_ 2. The criterion is 5 seconds.

_✓_ 3. The criterion is feeding herself (without assistance).

_✓_ 4. The criterion is within 2 minutes after entering the classroom.

_____ 5. Without eating the soap? Within 5 minutes? Standing up?

Practice Set 1C

1. The objective has all three components.
2. Only the behavioral verb is specified.

3. Only the condition is specified.
4. The objective has all three components.
5. The criterion level is missing.
6. The objective has all three components.

Review Set 1

1. observation
2. behavioral
3. criterion
4. conditions
5. time, repetitions, accuracy
6. simple
7. a. perform
   b. environment
   c. developmental
   d. achievable

Practice Set 2A

1. Mr. Rendleman saying "It is time to catch the bus."
2. the button
3. the big wheel
4. the needle
5. the candy

Practice Set 2B

1. Stimulus: The presence of Judy's mother
   Response: Judy *crying*

2. Stimulus: Ms. Klein telling Adam to stop pinching Sandy
   Response: Adam *falling* to the floor

3. Stimulus: The aide putting a spoon near Mary's mouth
   Response: Mary *opening* her mouth

4. Stimulus: The water in the toilet
   Response: Nate *drinking* from the toilet

Practice Set 2C

1. Stimulus: Toys
   Response: Mindy *throwing* toys

Consequence: Mindy's hands being held by the instructor

2. Stimulus: Daniel's teacher asking for the toy
   Response: Daniel *handing* his teacher the toy
   Consequence: Daniel's teacher telling him he is a good boy

3. Stimulus: The scab on Helen's hand
   Response: Helen *picking* the scab
   Consequence: The instructor telling Helen to stop picking her scab

4. Stimulus: The paper cup
   Response: Marvin *throwing* the paper cup
   Consequence: Marvin sitting in the corner

5. Stimulus: The paint brush
   Response: Richard *mouthing* the paint brush
   Consequence: The instructor rinsing out Richard's mouth with water

Practice Set 2D

____✔____ 1. The consequences in this situation were both reinforcing and punishing. Eating the crackers was reinforcing, since that behavior was repeated many times; having the box taken away was punishing, since Patrice cried and regurgitated as a result. (Punishing consequences will be discussed next.)

_____ 2. The consequence in this situation was not reinforcing. Sammy didn't receive the attention he had sought by placing puzzle pieces in his mouth, and stopped engaging in the behavior.

____✔____ 3. The consequence in this situation was reinforcing because Mary liked chocolate pie and requested another piece.

____✔____ 4. The consequence in this situation was reinforcing because Jerry took five more steps after he received a drink of his favorite soda pop.

Practice Set 2E

____✔____ 1. The consequence in this situation, brushing Ann's teeth with Listerine, was punishing. We know this because Ann stopped trying to eat paste and because she cried during the toothbrushing.

_____ 2. The consequence in this situation, requiring Patrick to apologize, wasn't punishing and, in fact, appeared to be reinforcing, since his rate of spitting had increased.

_____ 3. The consequence in this situation was punishing. James cried and didn't attempt to tear the wheels off the new toy truck.

_____ 4. The consequence in this situation, being left alone, wasn't punishing and, in fact, appeared to be reinforcing since Denise seemed quite happy playing by herself.

Practice Set 2F

1. Stimuli: A surprise busy box and a verbal instruction

   Response: Sally will *turn* the dial on the busy box.

   Reinforcing Consequence: Your choice can be an object, edible, happening, person, or anything else that Sally likes and finds reinforcing. This item may then be used to reinforce turning the dial. For example, Sally will be reinforced for turning the dial on the box by receiving a bite of an animal cracker.

2. Stimuli: Loose fitting pants placed on Jeffrey, a verbal instruction, and physical guidance of Jeffrey's hands if necessary

   Response: Jeffrey will *raise* his pants from the hip.

   Reinforcing Consequence: An object, edible, happening, person, or anything else that Jeffrey likes and finds reinforcing can be used as a reinforcing consequence.

3. Stimuli: Toothbrush, pleasant-tasting toothpaste, a verbal instruction, and physical guidance in toothbrushing if necessary

   Response: Beverly will *brush* the front surface of her teeth.

   Reinforcing Consequence: An object, edible, happening, person, or anything else that Beverly likes and finds reinforcing can be used as a reinforcing consequence. Hint: You might try a battery-powered toothbrush, since vibration is often a reinforcing consequence for retarded students. (See Chapter 3 for warnings on the use of vibration with students who have cerebral palsy.)

4. Stimuli: Someone holding Richard's favorite toy or treat who is sitting 6 feet away from him and a verbal instruction

Response: Richard will *wheel* his wheelchair 6 feet.

Reinforcing Consequence: An object, edible, happening, person, or anything else that Richard likes and finds reinforcing can be used as a reinforcing consequence.

5. Stimuli: A two-handled cup filled with a beverage, a verbal instruction, and placement of Reed's hands on the cup if necessary

Response: Reed will *drink* from a two-handled cup.

Reinforcing Consequence: An object, edible, happening, person, or anything else that Reed likes and finds reinforcing can be used as a reinforcing consequence. If you select the beverage that the student most enjoys, then drinking from the cup will be reinforced by obtaining a drink.

Review Set 2

1. stimulus, response, consequence
2. stimulus
3. response
4. consequence
5. reinforcing, punishing
6. reinforcing
7. reinforcer
8. reinforcement
9. punishing
10. punisher
11. punishment
12. response, stimulus, reinforcing
13. consequence
14. response, reinforcing

Practice Set 3A

1. a. Yes in both cases
   b. No
   c. Rita was probably thirsty from the 10 bits of pretzels she had received. An appropriate reinforcer at 10:17 a.m. would have been a liquid reinforcer such as water. In fact, Rita was indicating her preference for this reinforcer by pointing to the water fountain.
2. a. A social reinforcer

     b. Yes. Ms. Elliot should have paired an edible reinforcer (something that Barbara is known to like to eat) with the social reinforcer. Also, Ms. Elliot should have named the behavior she was reinforcing, saying something like "Good, you're standing in the walker."

     c. Since Barbara was a new student, she should be given an edible and a social reinforcer simultaneously. A new instructor is unlikely to be socially reinforcing for a student right away. Furthermore, you should make sure before the training starts that the reinforcers to be used are ones that Barbara will respond for.

3. a. A tactile reinforcer

     b. No. Physical touch isn't harmful. Furthermore, if Bart had been tactually defensive, Ms. Quigley would have known immediately by his behavior.

     c. Yes. Ms. Quigley should have consulted a physical therapist because vibratory stimulation may not be appropriate for some students with certain physical problems, such as some forms of cerebral palsy or contracted or constricted muscles.

Practice Set 3B

1. Since Don is verbal, the most expedient way of determining some new reinforcers would be to ask him what he would like to have as reinforcers.

2. Mr. Douglas should observe students who are very similar to Clare. If that isn't successful, he may wish to try reinforcer sampling.

3. Ms. George could use the behavior William performs frequently to reinforce the behavior he performs infrequently. Thus, Ms. George would reinforce William by allowing him to rock briefly (for maybe 15 seconds) after he hands her a requested object.

Review Set 3

1. edible
2. edible, liquids
3. satiation
4. deprivation
5. apron
6. immediately

7. tactile, vibratory, auditory, olfactory
8. sensory
9. physical therapist
10. social
11. paired
12. potential
13. ask
14. observe
15. similar
16. Premack Principle
17. reinforcer sampling
18.

Edibles	Sensory	Social
M & M	Vibration to the student's neck	A hug (could also be sensory)
Kool-Aid	Stroking the student's face with your hand	A kiss (could also be sensory)
Water	Bouncing the student on your knee	A smile
Popcorn	Rubbing the student's feet with your hand	A nod
Milk	A back rub	A glance
	A Strauss waltz	
	A spinning top	
	The odor of peppermint	

Practice Set 4A

1. No. It is true that to create an appropriate environment for the one-to-one instructional model, you must have learning areas within the classroom or instructional area that are devoid of distractors. However, the classroom should be an exciting, stimulating place. Thus, pictures and toys in the classroom are highly desirable.

2. The correct answer is Classroom C. One student is receiving one-to-one instruction in a distraction-free environment while the remaining students stay in a group. There is no one-to-one instruction in Classroom A. Classroom B has toys in the one-to-one training area. In Classroom D, the student receiving one-to-one instruction from the teacher is out in the classroom where he could be distracted.

3. The correct answer is Classroom B. Two students are each receiving one-to-one instruction in distraction-free areas while two groups of students are each being supervised by an aide. In Classroom A a partition does not separate the students receiving one-to-one instruction from their classmates, and these students also do not have their backs to the classroom. In Classroom C, the aide giving one-to-one instruction is not using a partition.

Practice Set 4B

1. William should be taken to the bathroom, shown the toilet, and then placed on it during a time when he normally does urinate. This process should be repeated several times throughout the day. After a day or so, William should adapt to the new toilet.

2. Ruth first should have the opportunity to play with or touch the leg brace and then wear it for very short periods of time.

3. Jeffrey should not receive instruction until he has had an opportunity to play in the classroom and interact with the students and instructors. When he begins to initiate interactions or appears to be calm, you can begin his instruction.

4. Before instructing the students, you will play with them and help the aide attend to the students' physical needs. In this fashion you'll learn about the students, your co-workers, and the unit routine.

5. Before beginning the eye contact training, Jason should be allowed to familiarize himself with his new surroundings. After Jason has spent some time looking around and touching the table and chairs, you may begin instructing him.

Practice Set 4C

_____   1. The lollipops were given contingent on being on the gym mat.

✔   2. All students received a pretzel stick regardless of their behavior.

✔   3. Mr. Thomas reads to Earl every night at 8:00 regardless of Earl's behaviors.

_____   4. Ms. Gwynn pushed Brian on the swing contingent on his hanging up his jacket.

_____   5. The lemonade was contingent on sitting and being quiet.

Review Set 4

1. distraction-free
2. one-to-one
3. adapt
4. noncontingent
5. noncontingent
6. reinforcing

Practice Set 5A

_____ 1. Mr. Smith gave all the children 25 cents independent of their behaviors. Therefore, he was using noncontingent reinforcement.

__✔__ 2. Mr. Smith only gave 25 cents to children who helped clean the yard. Therefore, he was using contingent reinforcement, since the response, yard cleaning, had to be performed in order to receive the reinforcer, 25 cents.

__✔__ 3. Ten points were contingent (dependent) on using the toilet.

__✔__ 4. Potato chips were contingent (dependent) on walking to the bus.

_____ 5. Popsicles were given to all students regardless or independent of their behaviors. Therefore, the Popsicles were delivered noncontingently, since the students didn't have to behave (do anything) in order to receive them.

Practice Set 5B

_____ 1. This is not an example of continuous reinforcement since Samuel wasn't reinforced for putting his dishes in the sink at breakfast.

__✔__ 2. This is an example of continuous reinforcement. Sally was reinforced for taking off her jacket each time the behavior occurred.

__✔__ 3. This is an example of continuous reinforcement. Ricky was reinforced each time he picked up his clothes.

_____ 4. Marilyn received continuous reinforcement the first week, but didn't receive continuous reinforcement the second week.

_✓_ 5. Jacques is receiving continuous reinforcement. Each time he sat up, he was reinforced.

Practice Set 5C

_____ 1. Joshua was reinforced for *every* response. This is continuous reinforcement.

_✓_ 2. Barbara was receiving intermittent reinforcement. Every fourth response was reinforced.

_✓_ 3. Steven was receiving intermittent reinforcement. He was reinforced every 5 minutes.

_____ 4. Nicholas received continuous reinforcement. He received a kiss *each* day.

_✓_ 5. Elizabeth received intermittent reinforcement. She cleaned her room 7 days and received reinforcement on 3 of the days.

Practice Set 5D

1. Jessica will be reinforced every third time she hands her teacher the correct object.
2. Alfred will receive a reinforcer each time he has placed five bolts in the box.
3. 3
4. 8

Practice Set 5E

1. 4 (3 + 6 + 4 + 3 = 16 ÷ 4 = VR 4)
2. 5 (8 + 3 + 7 + 2 = 20 ÷ 4 = VR 5)
3. Any answer is correct if the average number of stacked towels being reinforced is five.

Practice Set 5F

_✓_ 1. This is an example of a fixed interval schedule. The reinforcer (10 points) was contingent on a prespecified response (reading) occurring after a prespecified amount of time had elapsed (5 minutes).

_✓_ 2. This is an example of a fixed interval schedule. The

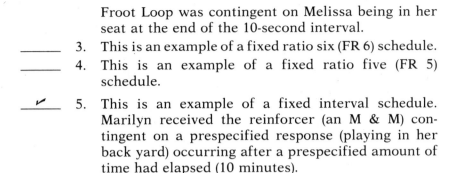

Froot Loop was contingent on Melissa being in her seat at the end of the 10-second interval.

____ 3. This is an example of a fixed ratio six (FR 6) schedule.

____ 4. This is an example of a fixed ratio five (FR 5) schedule.

✔ 5. This is an example of a fixed interval schedule. Marilyn received the reinforcer (an M & M) contingent on a prespecified response (playing in her back yard) occurring after a prespecified amount of time had elapsed (10 minutes).

Practice Set 5G

✔ 1. The reinforcer (happy face stickers) is being delivered at random intervals.

____ 2. This is an FI 3 minute schedule.

✔ 3. The visits and reinforcer (praise) are periodic and thereby random.

____ 4. It is a VR 4 schedule.

____ 5. 50 seconds (60 + 45 + 120 + 30 + 15 + 60 + 20 = 350 ÷ 7 = 50 seconds)

Review Set 5

1. noncontingent
2. contingent
3. contingent
4. continuous, intermittent
5. continuous
6. continuous
7. schedule
8. extinguishes
9. satiation
10. "wears," uses, generalization
11. intermittent
12. reinforcers
13. intermittent
14. ratio, response
15. interval, time
16. ratio

17. fixed, variable
18. fixed
19. pause
20. variable ratio
21. predictable
22. interval
23. fixed interval
24. pause
25. variable interval
26. predict
27. variable interval
28. random
29. variable interval

Practice Set 6

1. a. target
   b. initial
   c. reinforcers
   d. reinforce
   e. successive approximations
   f. reinforce
   g. intermittent
2. a. Laura independently eating with a spoon
   b. Laura grasping the spoon and scooping food
   c. 2 seconds of vibration and praise, i.e., "Good eating, Laura."
   d. Ms. Wolf will continue the vibration and praise until Laura meets some prespecified criterion level, e.g., successfully scooping on 4 of 5 (80%) feeding trials.
   e. A successive approximation occurs each time Laura moves the spoon closer to her mouth. Each successive approximation will be reinforced by the vibration and Ms. Wolf's praise.
   f. By a bite of food, the vibration, and Ms. Wolf's praise
   g. Self-feeding is unique in that the behavior is always reinforced continuously because each spoonful results in the reinforcer (a bite of food). However, Ms. Wolf can deliver her praise (the other reinforcer that would be maintaining self-feeding) on an intermittent schedule of reinforcement,

e.g., praising Laura after five successive independent bites.

3. criterion
4. observe

Review Set 6

1. shaping
2. new, repertoire
3. target
4. initial
5. response
6. a. discriminative
   b. guidance
   c. imitative
   d. fading

Practice Set 7A

1. A prompt is considered to be an auxiliary discriminative stimulus because it is given *in addition* to the naturally occurring discriminative stimuli that are associated with the behavior to be performed.
2. a. verbal
   b. physical
   c. gestural
   d. This is not a prompt; it is a natural discriminative stimulus.
   e. verbal
   f. gestural
   g. physical
3. fading
4. A prompt to which the student can respond successfully. In general, this will be a very obvious prompt.
5. Reducing the number of words or speaking progressively more softly
6. Progressively reducing the size of the gesture or changing to a less obvious gesture
7. a. Progressively reducing the amount of touch that you use
   b. Progressively reducing the amount of pressure associated with the touch that you use

   c. Progressively moving your touch (the physical prompt) away from the part of the student's body or area that is being prompted
   d. Using physical prompts with the other two types of prompts and fading the physical prompt first
8. Yes. She used a verbal prompt, "Hand me the sock," and a physical prompt, guiding Marvin's hand to the sock.

Practice Set 7B

1. The correct sequence is d, c, a, e, b, g, f.
2. Ms. Tuttle should hold the edible by her mouth but hidden from view. Over successive speech trials, she should raise the edible to her chin, to her throat, to her chest, to her side, and end by taking the edible directly from the bowl and placing it in George's mouth following an appropriate utterance.
3. No. He should start by using the prompts that had been successful the previous day.
4. It's a bad idea because in any training session you should never return to a prompt that has been faded. Mr. Pares could try a couple of different strategies. He could try a different edible reinforcer and hold it so that Sidney could see it. He also could give a very slight gestural prompt such as pointing down to the spot where he wanted Sidney to walk. It would be best if he tried both simultaneously.
5. Ms. Saunders did not stay within arm's reach of Ann even though she was in the initial stages of teaching her to brush her hair. Thus, she could not provide a physical prompt or guidance when Ann failed to respond to the verbal prompt.

Review Set 7

1. prompt
2. physical, verbal, gestural
3. fading
4. physical
5. prompter, prompts
6. obvious, active

Practice Set 8A

1. Touch his/her ear
   "Cindy, do this" or "Cindy, touch your ear"

Touch her ear
She'll receive reinforcement.
2. Clap his/her hands
"Sandy, do this" or "Sandy, clap your hands"
Clap her hands
She'll receive reinforcement.

Practice Set 8B

	Modeled Behavior	Imitated Behavior	Imitative Prompt	Other Prompts	Reinforcers
1.	lifting his arm	lifting her arm	"Do this."		gumdrop
2.	tapping the table	tapping the table	"Tap the table."	guiding Leon's hand	hug, bit of pecan
3.	rolling the ball	rolling the ball	"Do this."		vibration
4.	"Ka"	"Ka"	"Say 'Ka,' " forming the "k" sound with his lips		decaffeinated coffee

Review Set 8

1. imitative
2. imitation
3. generalized
4. imitative
5. model
6. reinforcement
7. previously, alternate, likes

Practice Set 9A

1. task analysis
2. order
3. from memory, by physically performing the task
4. You may omit a crucial detail or step.
5. a. Are you familiar with the objective?

   b. Is there a likelihood that you might omit a step or crucial detail?

   c. Is any special equipment or area needed?

Practice Set 9B

1. Responses: pick up spoon, scoop food onto spoon, raise spoon toward mouth, place spoon in mouth

   Discriminative stimuli: spoon beside plate of food, spoon in hand, food on spoon, spoon near mouth

   Terminal reinforcers: food, praise

2. S^D for scooping food onto spoon, Sr^+ for picking up the spoon

3. Task analysis for eating with a spoon:

   a. Pick up spoon

   b. Scoop food onto spoon

   c. Raise spoon toward mouth

   d. Place spoon in mouth

   You would use forward chaining since all the necessary self-feeding behaviors are in the student's behavioral repertoire.

4. You would use shaping.

5. Backward chaining. You would begin by teaching the last response in the self-feeding chain first. Accordingly, you would guide the student's hand so that the spoonful of food was very near his mouth. He would then eat the food and be praised. Next, you would guide the student's hand so that the spoonful of food was a little further away from his mouth. You would continue to move backwards in the response chain until the last response you taught would be picking up the spoon (the first response in the chain).

6. response, terminal, steps

7. forward, backward

8. prompting, imitative, fading, shaping, continuous reinforcement

Practice Set 9C

   I. Step 6 Pull his pants up to his *calves*

      Step 8 *Pull his pants up to his* buttocks

      Instruction should begin at Step 4.

   II. Instruction should begin at Step 2, since the student can place one sock on top of the other but does not put the socks heel to heel and toe to toe.

III. Step 2 *Remove* shampoo bottle cap

Step 7 Work shampoo into a *lather*

Step 12 *Dry hair* with towel

Instruction should begin at Step 1, since there is no indication that the student can remove the cap from the shampoo bottle.

IV. Instruction should begin at Step 1, since the student as yet does not know how to place his fingers and thumbs on the snaps.

V. Instruction should begin at Step 2.

VI. The behavioral objective: When instructed, the student will wet his toothbrush independently on 9 of 10 trials.

Step 1 Turn on the water

Step 4 Turn off the water

Instruction should begin at Step 2, since the student has never independently picked up his toothbrush.

Review Set 9

1. behavioral
2. sequence
3. entry
4. behavior chain
5. stimulus-response
6. terminal
7. conditioned
8. discriminative
9. discriminative stimulus, discriminative stimulus, conditioned reinforcer
10. S^D
11. S^{r+}
12. S^{R+}
13. responses
14. forward chaining, behavioral repertoire
15. first, last
16. backward chaining
17. last, first
18. perform
19. records, conversations, direct observation

Review Set 10

1. graduated guidance
2. full, partial, shadowing
3. verbal, physical
4. moment, moment
5. full
6. thumb, forefinger
7. shadowing
8. trial
9. force, force
10. praise
11. end
12. respond, trial
13. respond, within, avoidance
14. avoid, escape
15. physical guidance
16. backward chaining

Practice Set 11

1. a. 3 to 5, 3.8
   b. Yes
   c. No
   d. Yes. The baseline should be continued until the last base-line data point is the same as or lower than the previous day's data point. This is necessary because the purpose of the intervention is to increase the number of times that Susan will sit in her seat when requested to do so.
2. a. 0 to 2, 1.17
   b. Yes
   c. Yes
   d. No. The baseline is sufficient because enough records were taken to show that there are no wide fluctuations in Ross' operant level and the final baseline number was lower than the previous day, which means the behavior is not increasing.
3. 41.7% (5 ÷ 12 x 100)
4. a. 24 to 35, 29.2
   b. Yes

    c. Yes

    d. No. The baseline is sufficient for the same reasons specified in 2.

5. a. 10 to 68, 34.2

    b. No

    c. No

    d. Yes. The baseline should be continued until there are no wide fluctuations in Pat's percentage of in-seat behavior and the last baseline percentage is the same as or lower than the previous day's percentage.

Review Set 11

1. operant level
2. baseline
3. objective
4. tally, frequency counting
5. time sampling
6. range, data point

Practice Set 12A

1. Yes. The baseline was stable and the final baseline session's data point was as low or lower than the previous session's data point.
2. Yes. The number of times Betty sat down when instructed to do so by her teacher increased quickly.
3. Baseline average: .5 times per session (5 ÷ 10 = .5). Training average: 6.4 times per session (64 ÷ 10 = 6.4).
4. There was a 1280% increase in sitting down during the training program (6.4/.5 x 100 = 1280%).
5. Yes. The reinforcement program increased Betty's sitting down by 1280% after 10 training sessions, whereas the criterion level of success was a 300% increase.
6. Yes
7. Baseline average: 1 time per session (7 ÷ 7 = 1). Training average: 1 time per session (10 ÷ 10 = 1).
8. No. The criterion level for success of a 300% increase after 10 training sessions was not reached. The graph also shows that the reinforcement program had no effect.
9. She should try another reinforcement program.

Practice Set 12B

1. a. Yes
   b. Yes
2. a. 44%
   b. 90%
3. a. 77.8% (7 ÷ 9 x 100 = 77.8%)
   b. Observer 1, 50%; Observer 2, 38.9%
4. a. 12%
   b. 76%
   c. 533% (76 − 12 = 64 ÷ 12 x 100)
   d. Yes. Ms. Norton should continue to use the reinforcement procedure, since it increased Billy's saying the "Mm" sound to well above the 80% increase over the baseline average she had specified as meeting the criterion for success after five sessions.

Review Set 12

1. frequency
2. criterion
3. interobserver reliability
4. agreed, agreed, disagreed
5. lower, higher
6. 70%
7. criterion
8. graph
9. time sampling

Review Set 13

1. generalization training
2. discriminate
3. common, intermittent reinforcement, conditions, discriminative, reinforcement
4. behavior maintenance
5. naturally, train, fade, training, intermittent schedules, delay
6. complex, student, analyzed
7. expected, change, motivated, reinforcers, consistently
8. thyself, student, respects, fairness
9. arbitrarily, bias, systematic, help, performance

GLOSSARY

Adaptation: The phase in a behavioral program during which the student is allowed to adjust to novel stimuli in the new learning environment.

Attenuation: The process of gradually making a schedule of reinforcement more and more intermittent.

Auditory reinforcer: Any sounds (e.g., music) for which the student will respond.

Auxiliary discriminative stimulus: An added stimulus, such as a prompt, that accompanies other stimuli associated with reinforcement.

Avoidance learning: The learning that occurs when a response is made in order to avoid or escape something that is unpleasant.

Backward chaining: A procedure in which the last response in a behavior chain is taught first and the first response is taught last.

Baseline: The period of time during which a behavior is observed and measured without any intervention (training).

Behavior: Any observable and measurable act of the student. *See also* Response.

Behavior chain: A sequence of stimuli and responses that ends with a terminal reinforcer. It is also called a *stimulus-response chain*.

Behavior frequency: The number of times a behavior occurs during a specific period of time. *See also* Frequency counting.

Behavior maintenance: The degree to which a target behavior continues to occur after formal programming has been discontinued.

Behavioral approach: An approach to changing behavior based on direct observation and objective measurement of the student's behavior. It systematically uses methods and experimental findings from behavioral science.

Behavioral objective: A written statement that describes three things about an individual's performance of a behavior: (1) what the behavior is, (2) how much or how well it is done, and (3) the circumstances under which it is done. These three elements are expressed as (1) the behavioral verb, (2) the criterion level, and (3) the conditions.

Behavioral repertoire: The behaviors that a particular student, at a particular time, is capable of performing.

Behavioral verb: A description of the measurable behavior the student will be expected to perform. *See also* Behavioral objective.

Conditioned reinforcer: A previously neutral stimulus that has acquired its reinforcing properties from being repeatedly paired with a reinforcer.

Conditions: The circumstances in which a behavior is to be performed. *See also* Behavioral objective.

Consequence: The event that happens to the student after the response occurs. *See also* Instructional cycle.

Contingency: The relation between the response (the target behavior) and the consequence.

Contingent reinforcement: Reinforcement that depends upon a specific response.

Continuous recording: The recording of each behavior every time it occurs throughout the recording period.

Continuous reinforcement: The reinforcement of every occurrence of a response.

Criterion: A description of how much or how well a behavior is to be performed. It is also called a *criterion level*. Criteria are used to evaluate the success of a behavioral program. *See also* Behavioral objective.

Criterion level: *See* Criterion.

Deprivation: The state that occurs when a reinforcer has been withheld until it once again is effective in increasing or maintaining a behavior. It is the opposite of satiation.

Discrimination: The process of behaving one way in one situation and a different way in another situation.

Discriminative stimulus: A stimulus that sets the occasion for a response to occur because it has been associated with reinforcement.

Edible reinforcer: The foods preferred by the student.

Entry behaviors: Those behaviors that the student possesses before instruction begins.

Extinction: The withholding of the reinforcer that has been sustaining or increasing a behavior.

Fading: The gradual removal of a prompt.

FI: An abbreviation for fixed interval.

Fixed interval (FI) schedule: A schedule of reinforcement in which the reinforcer follows the first prespecified response after a prespecified amount of time has elapsed.

Fixed ratio (FR) schedule: A schedule of reinforcement in which the reinforcer follows a predetermined number of responses.

Forward chaining: A procedure in which the first response in a behavior chain is taught first and the last response is taught last.

FR: An abbreviation for fixed ratio.

Frequency counting: A recording method in which the number of times a behavior occurs during a specified period of time is tallied.

Full graduated guidance: The segment of a graduated guidance procedure in which the trainer physically guides the performance of the desired behavior.

Generalization: The occurrence of a particular behavior (or behaviors similar to it) in a situation in which training has not taken place.

Generalization training: A procedure for transferring control over behavior in one situation to other situations.

Generalized imitation: The occurrence of an imitated behavior that has not been previously reinforced.

Gestural prompt: A motor behavior (e.g., pointing) that is presented to cue the performance of a particular response.

Graduated guidance: A technique combining physical guidance and fading in which the physical guidance is systematically and gradually reduced and then faded completely. It has three parts: full graduated guidance, partial graduated guidance, and shadowing.

Imitation: The response of matching the behavior of a model.

Imitative prompt: A discriminative stimulus provided by a model in which the model's behavior is to be imitated.

Initial behavior: A behavior that the student performs before instruction begins and that resembles the target behavior in some way. It is the first behavior reinforced in a shaping procedure.

Instructional cycle: The stimulus, response, and consequence series. It is also called the *three-term contingency*.

Intermittent reinforcement: The reinforcement of some, but not all, occurrences of a response.

Interobserver reliability: A measure of the degree to which two or more observers agree that a specific behavior occurred.

Interval schedule of reinforcement: A reinforcement schedule based on the interval of time between reinforced responses. There are two kinds of interval schedules: fixed interval and variable interval.

Intervention: The action that is taken to change a target behavior.

Learning history: The sum of an individual's behaviors that have been conditioned or modified as a result of environmental events. It is also called a *reinforcement history*.

Manual guidance: *See* Physical guidance.

Modeling: The presentation of a behavior to be imitated. *See also* Imitation.

Natural consequence: A consequence that is not programmed but rather is provided by the environment.

Noncontingent reinforcement: Reinforcement that is not related to any specific response.

Olfactory reinforcer: A pleasant-smelling substance (e.g., a scratch-and-sniff book) for which the student will respond.

One-to-one instructional model: An instructional situation in which only the student and a teacher or aide are present.

Operant behavior: A behavior that is controlled by its consequences.

Operant level: A description of the frequency of a behavior before instruction begins.

Partial graduated guidance: The segment of a graduated guidance procedure in which the trainer fades the amount of physical guidance so that the student gradually performs the desired behavior with less assistance.

Physical guidance: The guidance of the performance of a behavior using constant and continuous physical contact. It is also called *manual guidance*.

Physical prompt: Any form of physical contact between the trainer and the student that is presented to cue the performance of a particular response.

Positive reinforcement: The delivery of a positive reinforcer contingent upon a response or behavior.

Positive reinforcer: A stimulus that, when presented as a consequence of a behavior, results in an increase or maintenance of that behavior.

Potential punisher: An event that is presumed to act as a punisher. It cannot be said to be a punisher until it has decreased the future performance of a behavior it follows.

Potential reinforcer: An event that is presumed to act as a reinforcer. It cannot be said to be a reinforcer until it has increased the future performance of a behavior it follows.

Premack Principle: A procedure in which a behavior the student performs frequently is used to reinforce a behavior the student seldom performs.

Prompt: An auxiliary discriminative stimulus that is presented to cue the student to perform a specified behavior. Prompts are usually faded before the terminal behavior has been achieved. There are three types of prompts: verbal, gestural, and physical.

Punisher: Any event that decreases the future probability of the response it follows. It is also called a *punishing consequence*.

Punishing consequence: *See* Punisher.

Punishment: A procedure that decreases the future probability of a behavior.

R: An abbreviation for response.

Ratio schedule of reinforcement: A reinforcement schedule based on the number of responses that are performed. There are two kinds of ratio schedules: fixed ratio and variable ratio.

Reinforcement: A procedure that maintains or increases the future probability of a behavior.

Reinforcement density: The frequency or rate at which responses are reinforced.

Reinforcement history: *See* Learning history.

Reinforcement schedule: *See* Schedule of reinforcement.

Reinforcer: Any event that maintains or increases the future probability of the response it follows. It is also called a *reinforcing consequence*.

Reinforcer sampling: A procedure whereby the student tries a variety of potential reinforcers.

Reinforcing consequence: *See* Reinforcer.

Response: The behavior the student performs in the presence of a particular stimulus. *See also* Instructional cycle.

Satiation: The state that occurs when a reinforcer has been presented to the point that it is no longer effective in increasing or maintaining a behavior. It is the opposite of deprivation.

Schedule of reinforcement: A description of when a reinforcer will be delivered. It is also called a *reinforcement schedule.*

S^D: An abbreviation for discriminative stimulus.

Sensory reinforcer: Any sensations that the student likes or enjoys. Sensory reinforcers include tactile, vibratory, olfactory, visual, and auditory reinforcers.

Shadowing: The segment of a graduated guidance procedure in which the amount of physical guidance has been faded to the point that the trainer has no physical contact with the student, but is prepared to reapply full or partial graduated guidance should the behavior slow down or stop.

Shaping: The reinforcement of successive approximations of a target behavior to produce a behavior that is currently not in the student's behavioral repertoire.

Social reinforcer: A smile, praise, attention, or friendly remarks that the student likes or enjoys.

S^{r+}: An abbreviation for conditioned reinforcer.

S^{R+}: An abbreviation for terminal reinforcer.

Stimulus: Any physical object or occurrence in the environment that may set the occasion for a response to occur. Stimuli frequently used in behavioral programs include reinforcing stimuli, aversive stimuli, and discriminative stimuli. *See also* Instructional cycle.

Stimulus-response chain: *See* Behavior chain.

Successive approximations: A series of responses that more and more closely resemble the specified target behavior.

Tactile reinforcer: Any type of skin-to-skin contact between the trainer and the student for which the student will respond.

Target behavior: A desired behavior that does not occur or that occurs infrequently that we wish to establish or increase. It is also called a *terminal behavior.* In a behavioral reduction program, it is the inappropriate behavior that is to be decreased or eliminated.

Task analysis: A detailed description of each behavior needed to accomplish a behavioral objective given the student's current ability level.

Terminal behavior: *See* Target behavior.

Terminal reinforcer: The reinforcer at the end of a behavior (stimulus-response) chain.

Three-term contingency: *See* Instructional cycle.

Time sampling: A recording method in which the student is observed at fixed intervals (e.g., every 5 minutes) for a specified period of time (e.g., 30 seconds) and the occurrence or absence of a behavior during each interval is recorded.

Variable interval (VI) schedule: A schedule of reinforcement in which the reinforcer follows the first prespecified response after different intervals of time have elapsed such that over time a specific average interval is maintained.

Variable ratio (VR) schedule: A schedule of reinforcement in which the reinforcer follows a different number of responses each time such that over time a specific average number of responses is reinforced.

Verbal prompt: A verbalization, usually an instruction (e.g., "Look at me"), that is presented to cue the performance of a particular response.

VI: An abbreviation for variable interval.

Vibratory reinforcer: A period of stimulation applied with a vibrator for which the student will respond.

Visual reinforcer: Any type of visual stimulation (e.g., a color wheel) for which the student will respond.

VR: An abbreviation for variable ratio.

INDEX

ABOUT THE AUTHOR

Photo by Lynn Sequoia Ellner

Dr. Foxx is Director of Treatment Development at the Anna Mental Health and Developmental Center in Anna, Illinois, and an adjunct professor in the Rehabilitation Institute at Southern Illinois University at Carbondale. He has written 4 books and dozens of scientific articles, and has made 12 training films on the use of behavioral principles to treat normal, retarded, emotionally disturbed, and autistic individuals. He also is the developer of the technique of overcorrection. Dr. Foxx has consulted at institutions, schools, and community-based facilities across the United States and in Canada, Great Britain, Puerto Rico, and Haiti. He is on the editorial board of eight scientific journals and is the consulting editor for Research Press special education publications. One of his books, *Toilet Training in Less Than a Day*, has sold over a million copies and has been translated into seven languages, and one of his training films, *Harry* (the treatment of a self-abusive man), has won numerous cinematic awards.

Living Stones